STO

ACPL ITEM
DISCARDED

11·7·79

HOW TO CURE
YOUR JOGGERMANIA!

ALSO BY *Peter J. Steincrohn,* M.D., F.A.C.P.

How to Stop Killing Yourself
The Doctor Looks at Life
How to Be Lazy, Healthy and Fit
You Live as You Breathe
How to Get a Good Night's Sleep
Your Heart Is Stronger than You Think
Mr. Executive: Keep Well—Live Longer
Common Sense Coronary Care and Prevention
Live Longer and Enjoy It
You Can Increase Your Heart Power
Your Life to Enjoy
How to Master Your Nerves, Tension and Fatigue (Coauthor:
    David J. LaFia, M.D.)
Heart Worry and Its Cure
What You Can Do for High Blood Pressure
How to Master Your Fears
What You Can Do for Angina Pectoris and Coronary
    Occlusion
How to Keep Fit without Exercise
How to Add Years to Your Life
Heart Disease Is Curable
More Years for the Asking
Ask Dr. Steincrohn
Don't Die before Your Time
Antidotes for Anxiety
Low Blood Sugar
Questions and Answers about Nerves

HOW TO CURE YOUR JOGGERMANIA!

Enjoy Fitness and Good Health
without Running

Peter Steincrohn, M.D.

South Brunswick and New York: A. S. Barnes and Company
London: Thomas Yoseloff Ltd

© 1979 by A. S. Barnes and Co., Inc.

A. S. Barnes and Co., Inc.
Cranbury, New Jersey 08512

Thomas Yoseloff Ltd
Magdalen House
136-148 Tooley Street
London SE1 2TT, England

Library of Congress Cataloging in Publication Data

Steincrohn, Peter Joseph, 1899-
    How to cure your joggermania!

    Bibliography: p.
    1. Exercise. 2. Jogging—Physiological aspects.
3. Health. 4. Physical fitness. I. Title.
RA781.S76   613.7   79-51020
ISBN 0-498-02430-X

Printed in the United States of America

Dedicated to the underactive MAJORITY
who remain deliciously, incurably, incorrigibly lazy
as they gain refreshment from idle relaxation
in spite of the scornful, lofty, proclamations of the overactive MINORITY
who boastfully pretend that the creaks and squeaks
of weary, aching bones are worthy testament
that their monotonous, fatiguing, bizarre efforts
guarantee fitness and good health.

CONTENTS

Nobody can say an unfriendly word against the sheer goodness of keeping fit, but we should go careful with the promises.
—Lewis Thomas, M.D.
New England Journal of Medicine, August 31, 1978

> A vicarious pleasure
> of the physically lazy.
> OBSERVING others as they
> strain, push, and pull.
>   —Steincrohn

NOTE

Are you a jogger?

If so, are you aware of what you are doing? Why you are doing it? Only awareness can save you from uncomfortable and possibly serious complications.

Therefore, before reading this book I suggest that you ask yourself the following questions:

- Who influenced you to jog? Your doctor? An associate? A friend? Something you've read?
- Do you dislike being called lazy? Do you want to change your image?
- Are you overweight and do you want to reduce?
- Are you convinced that jogging will make you fit?
- Are you seeking a cure for insomnia? For something to reduce tension and depression?
- Do you think jogging will help you quit smoking?
- If you have hypertension, do you believe that jogging will bring your blood pressure down to normal?
- Are you certain that jogging will lessen the chance of heart attack? That it will provide good health and longevity?
- Have you asked yourself whether you really like jogging? Or whether you hate it?
- Have shin splints, backaches, or other more serious complications lessened your enthusiasm?
- When did you last have a complete medical checkup, if ever?

- If you are over 35, have you ever had a stress test?
- Does jogging tire you or increase your vim?
- Have you ever jogged and quit? Why? Did you start again? Why?
- Most important of all: Are you a potential jogger? My advice is? Don't begin. Like smoking, it's easier to begin than to quit.

Examine your self-portrait carefully. Once you ascertain your motivation for jogging or for not jogging, you will more clearly understand what I have to say in this book.

On his TV show one evening, Dick Cavett jestingly asked Robert Morley, "Do you believe in exercise? Do you jog?"

Morley, 70 and overweight answered, "I get my exercise walking from table to table. So many Americans are running. I think a lot of doctors are running up quite a bit of business. Joggers are getting blood in their urine, dying in bathtubs, or toppling over five minutes after sitting down. Jogging? Not for me."

You might say, "Why choose Robert Morley as a judge? This British actor looks like he's at least one hundred pounds overweight. What does he know about fitness and good health?"

Well, he has reached 70, fat or not. You can feel sure he has reached this respectable destination because he has had the innate wisdom to remain physically lazy and has refused to be influenced to exercise against his nature. If he had exercised, he might be too dead to talk about the dangers of jogging.

Let's hear from a doctor. I received the following note recently:

Dear Dr. Steincrohn:
    It is wonderful to hear from a doctor with some sense about exercise. From 1937 to 1976 I was engaged in the reeducation of doctors at the University of Tennessee College of Medicine.
    For all those years I kept pounding at them that there was not an iota of proof that exercise ever lengthened any person's life—and it has, in fact, prematurely ended some lives.
    There were some exceptions, I told them. For example, the exercise involved in digging a fox hole or running from a determined and armed adversary—these would be considered in the category of life-saving exercises.

I can get enough exercise by walking to the dining room. I am 82 years old and to my knowledge never did an honest days work involving other than mental activity in my entire life.

Frank L. Roberts, M.D.

Rationality requires honest, impartial self-examination. I'll help you make your decisions whether to jog, quit—or not begin.

P.J.S.

FOREWORD

In private, and in the public media, I have often expressed my frank opinions about jogging. I have been amused by the astonishment of TV-program moderators and newspaper interviewers whenever I have said that I do not consider that jogging is helpful to the heart—or that it is life-prolonging. At times it may even be harmful.

I agree with Dr. Steincrohn that joggitis has become an epidemic. Millions of persons are expending their energy needlessly. With sheeplike credulity, they attempt to attain physical fitness and good health by overexerting.

Dr. Steincrohn's HOW TO CURE YOUR JOGGERMANIA! will help convince lazy persons that they do *not* need to jog. It will also help reluctant joggers, who want a good excuse, to quit. And I believe it will show those who suffer from joggermania how to overcome their addiction. (It is indeed a Mania).

Dr. Steincrohn makes an excellent point in saying that "If you're pushing 40, that's exercise enough." He also makes good sense in suggesting that "the best thing to exercise is *discretion*."

For many years I've also advocated moderate forms of exertion such as walking, golfing, swimming, gardening. I believe that the heart muscle appreciates such mild exercise; rather than bursts of physical over-activity that send the pulse bounding, raise the blood pressure, while the jogger pants for breath.

If you read Dr. Steincrohn's book you will "jog with care" if you still jog. Or, you will quit, without having to make any excuses to your doctor or friends. Dr. Steincrohn will show you how to become fit without jogging. One way or another, you will have been cured of JOGGERMANIA!

Christiaan N. Barnard, M.D.

PREFACE

What is the best kind of exercise? Other than walking, which I believe in, I facetiously recommend bicycle riding, downhill.

My conscience can't rest unless I come out periodically against the oracular opinions of those who seem to think than exercise is one of the greatest weapons against coronary disease, that it is one of the cheapest premiums for life insurance and longevity.

What set off a firecracker under me today was reading the statement by one of our foremost scientists and respected physicians: "Studies prove the value of regular exercise as a means of combating the rise of cholesterol and, presumably, of coronary disease. Exercise, to be of the most value, should be pushed to the limit. And it must be regular."

Out of similar statements was the epidemic of jogging born and nurtured.

I disagree on two points. First, I do not believe that it has been scientifically proved that exercise prevents coronary heart disease. There are too many other contributory factors, like obesity, high blood pressure, heredity, tension, heavy smoking and drinking—and the simple fact of being a male.

And second, I consider that exercise "pushed to the limit" causes more coronary attacks than it prevents. To begin exercising strenuously thinking it will prevent you from getting a heart attack is to place yourself in greater danger than if you decided to relax in a rocking chair or a hammock.

Think of how many, influenced by the statement "Exercise to be of any value should be pushed to the limit," will go right out to partake of large gobs of physical exertion without even having a physical examination to learn if they are able to withstand such exertions. There are many men and women pushing themselves "to the limit" completely unaware that their coronary arteries are in no condition to cope with the strain.

Generally speaking, my formula to prevent coronary attacks is not to smoke, be fortunate in your ancestry, stay within normal weight limits, tend to your blood pressure, manage diabetes if present, and learn to live without too much tension. Learning how to relax is more essential than pushing yourself to exercise.

Peace of mind plus physical moderation are the necessary ingredients in the formula for preventing a coronary attack. They are the most reliable prescription for keeping fit and healthy.

I reacted with consternation after reading a dispatch from the Associated Press:

> President Jimmy Carter is now a jogger. His physician, Rear Admiral William M. Lukash—a jogger himself—has undoubtedly recommended the President's physical regime. At the age of 54 our chief executive is taking it very seriously. He does his jogging on the oval driveway around the South Lawn of the White House, covering eight laps (two miles) in sixteen minutes. He jogs about three times a week at the White House; and also runs along the paths at Camp David.

Now, why should I be concerned about the president's fitness program? After all, how about Senator William Proxmire? Isn't he a perfect example of how jogging pays off? He has survived jogging. But others haven't.

Another dispatch from Sharpsburg, Maryland, reported that U. S. Representative Goodloe Byron, considered one of the best athletes in Congress, died of a heart attack while jogging. He was 49. A veteran of six Boston Marathons, Byron had jogged 12½ miles of a planned fifteen-mile outing along the Potomac when stricken. His aide, Brenton Ayer, said Byron "wasn't breathing hard and looked fine" before he collapsed. Byron had slowed but resumed jogging just before he stumbled and collapsed.

I can hear a chorus of protests: "Good Lord! You don't believe that the president's doctors would allow him to jog before he had a stress test?"

He was undoubtedly tested. Yet, this isn't the final answer. A doctor's letter in the *New England Journal of Medicine* put it well: "The current jogging craze has presented physicians with new and unusual medical problems." The August 24, 1978 edition of *Connecticut Medicine* (Morris L. Rossman, D. O., Robert Catvejai, D. O.) contains the following observations on exercise texts before exercise:

> Exercise for the sake of cardiovascular fitness has virtually become a national obsession in the United States. Many people who want to start an exercise program first seek the advice of a physician. The American College of Sports Medicine recommends an exercise test before any major increase in physical activity for all persons over 35 years of age, and for those under 35 with risk factors for coronary artery disease, including obesity, family history, cigarette smoking, hyperlipidemia, or hypertension.

(Abstract from American College of Sports Medicine Guidelines for Guarded Exercise Testing and Exercise Prescription: Lea and Febiger, Philadelphia, 1975)

The article further points out—and this is what concerns me about President Carter's recent membership in the jogging fraternity—that "the main objective of exercise testing (sometimes called stress testing) is to diagnose previously undetected coronary artery disease."

> A negative exercise test, on the other hand, may cause some people to dangerously overestimate their capacity for exercise. Stress tests give false-negative results in many patients with serious coronary artery disease demonstrable by angiography, even when they have angina pectoris. In one study of patients with coronary artery disease documented by angiography, exercise tests were normal in 60 percent of patients with single-vessel disease, 34 percent of those with double-vessel disease, and 24 percent of patients with triple-vessel disease. . . .

The results of exercise tests for asymptomatic people undertaking exercise programs are sometimes misleading. False-positive and false-negative results occur commonly, and can lead to serious consequences.

Call me an exercise nihilist, a joy killer, but reread what I have just quoted and you will understand why I felt immediate concern when I read that President Carter, had begun a jogging program. After Mr. Carter had been in office a couple of years, didn't you hear people saying, "Watch Carter's face on TV. Isn't it strained? Doesn't he look much older?" True, and so was his heart older. Unfortunately, in spite of all our modern scientific instruments, we can't surely measure the "look" of President Carter's heart as well as we can his face.

For fitness, Mr. President, I recommend sixteen minutes in a rocking chair rather than a sixteen-minute jog around the track.

INTRODUCTION

If you're pushing 40 that's exercise enough.

Keep remembering: The best thing to exercise is discretion.

In this book I'll offer you many ways to attain fitness without jogging. You will be able to enjoy relaxation and good health in a hammock or rocking chair. And you'll do it with a free conscience, even as you watch others jog by.

I do not agree with the generally accepted opinion that jogging will control or overcome anxiety, depression, hatreds, aggression, and hostility and that, in consequence, it will indirectly prevent diabetes, heart disease, hypertension, and stroke. There is no proof that jogging will prevent heart attacks, prolong youthfulness, and engender longevity.

Unfortunately, thousands of physicians, themselves addicted to jogging, continue to promulgate the theory that daily exertion is essential for good health. As a result, the grunting, perspiring bodies of their misguided patients churn the atmosphere throughout the United States. Is it any wonder that countless legs, arms, and torsos are contorting, straining, pushing, and pulling, while jogging, weight-lifting, doing pushups, swinging clubs, and crowding the gyms?

If you are a reluctant jogger, reading *How to Cure Your Joggermania!* will help you regain your composure and your peace of mind. I will help you withstand the pressures from doctors, family, friends, and business associates who may have become exercise zealots.

If you are physically lazy, stay physically lazy. Let Mother Nature guide you against unnatural physical activity.

Exercise-minded people often react like a bigoted minority. They rise to taunt the majority, who are physically lazy and thrive on relaxation. If you are a nonjogger, they may look upon you with a mixture of pity and contempt.

Joggermania will teach you how to deal with them. You will learn that if you don't run with the crowd, you're liable to be trampled on. Some angry joggers may even go out of their way to overturn your hammock or cut down the legs of your rocking chair.

For years I have been advocating forms of exertion like walking, golfing, tennis, bowling, swimming, gardening, hiking, or even doing a few minutes of setting up exercises—all in moderation. But jogging enthusiasts tell us that such exertions are of little value in maintaining fitness or promoting good health. Jog—or else!

Internationally recognized cardiologist Irvin S. Wright, M.D., writing in Medical World News (1/9/78), had these words of caution against overexertion.

A lot of factors should be considered. When people start on vigorous exercise, especially jogging, they may strain their knees and have a good deal of pain. They may develop foot problems, or they may be doing more than is good for their hearts.

It's fine for young people who are perfectly healthy to keep up on vigorous exercise, but there have been serious accidents when people start jogging after age 50.

Even if they get a stress test beforehand, it may just give them a false sense of security. Joggers can have heart attacks in gyms. What if it happens on a lonely country road?

Overexercise is a waste of God-given energy. There is much more to achieving fitness in life than simple physical fitness. I leave that to the young who are developing their bodies and to professional athletes. Is it necessary for you to revert to the physical needs required of your ancestors who lived in caves? Who lived when survival depended more on muscles than on brains? I'd like to see some of the joggermania siphoned off to produce mental fitness.

Do you believe that "mania" is too strong a word? The *American*

Heritage Dictionary defines "mania" as "an inordinately intense enthusiasm; craze." A maniac it says is "one who has an excessive enthusiasm for something." I can think of no more apt definition of jogging and its masochistic adherents. Calling jogging an "inordinately intense enthusiasm" is putting it kindly. It is a craze. And, following the dictionary definition, too many Americans have become maniacs in their devotion to this puzzling phenomenon.

However, in this enlightened scientific world, even mania is susceptible to improvement and cure, and in this book, I hope I can convince some joggers to fight free of their addiction. Even more important, I hope to keep the consciences of the physically lazy free, so they won't succumb to the importunities of their more active associates.

I will demonstrate that there is much that the medical profession still does not know about exercise. More important, I will show you how to be fit and healthy without torturing muscles that beg to be moderately active. More often than not, physical laziness should be worn as a badge of glory, rather than a badge of shame.

Be thankful that you have been blessed with constitutional inertia, or, euphemisms aside, that you have been born plain lazy.

HOW TO CURE
YOUR JOGGERMANIA!

PART 1
THE PROBLEM

1
THE "X" IN EXERCISE: KILL OR CURE?

Exercise has become the "in" thing to do. If you don't jog, pedal, or play golf or tennis, you're "out." "Unless you exert daily," say the exercise proponents, "you're a prime candidate for a heart attack."

It's time for a few kind words in behalf of those mavericks who refuse to lie down and be branded by the "X" in exercise—and, incidentally, for a strong word of caution and warning for those who exercise in search of fitness and who, as a result, may be in greater danger than their neighbor who underexercises.

Over 25 years of medical experience as an internist and cardiologist has not convinced me that exercise is unquestionably good for you, whether you are apparently well or have already suffered a heart attack. It must be granted that at times regular exercise will lower blood pressure and pulse rate and increase the output of the heart. However, no doctor has the unequivocal answer to whether exercise will reduce the risk of your having a heart attack or promote your longevity. That can come only with time. Dr. Victor F. Froelicher, Jr., formerly of the U.S. Air Force School of Aerospace Medicine, after reviewing eighty-five of the most important papers on the subject of exercise and cardiovascular health, reported that the evidence, though suggestive, was far from conclusive.

Before sitting down to the exertion of writing this book I knew that I'd have at least two classes of potential readers: millions of physically lazy persons who want a good excuse not to jog; and also the hundreds of thousands of reluctant joggers who want a good excuse to quit.

There is also a third group—those who have been reading my nationally syndicated column "Stop Killing Yourself" these past twenty-five years. This group consists of the large number of daily readers from every section of the United States and Canada who have sent me letters either agreeing or disagreeing with my consistently held view, that overexertion is a prodigious waste of God-given energy. I know that many of them are naturally curious to know what I have put between the covers of a book, rather than into the restricted space of my columns, regarding exercise.

Included in this group are many doctors who think that excessive exertion—especially jogging—is essential for fitness, good health, and longevity. In so believing, they have influenced millions of their patients to "jog for their health."

I'm trying to put a stop to the unfounded notions about jogging, and if you're a jogger, I ask you to clear your mind of any prejudices, both your own and those implanted in you by your physician and friends. Otherwise, what I say here will be wasted on you.

You are invited to sit and judge whatever evidence I present against jogging. Your decision about the usefulness of such exertions will depend upon your ability to step outside yourself and see yourself clearly. I trust your decision will be just and true, uninfluenced by any fear, hope, or vanity engendered by the prevailing exercise epidemic.

After you have read this book, I promise that you will jog "with care" if you still jog or that you will quit without having to make any excuses to your doctor or friends. Others, of course, will continue to enjoy (if physically lazy) their rocking chairs and hammocks without any qualms of conscience.

One way or another, I promise that you will have been cured of joggermania!

It is not necessary for you to revert to the physical exertions required when survival depended more on muscles than on brain. You can be fit and healthy without torturing muscles that beg and plead to be only moderately active. Like the healthy horse whipped to overwork day after day, you are likely to become old before your time if you overexert. Jogging until your heart beats so hard you actually pant for breath is not, in my opinion, a rational way to become fit.

The blame for the widespread epidemic of "exercisitis" or "joggitis" rests squarely with doctors. Following their advice, millions of patients have taken to beating their feet on pavement and country roads to the tune of pounding hearts. A few so-called "authorities" claim that jogging is the cure-all, and thousands of doctors enthusiastically approve of these daily physical gyrations.

The burden of proof is on those who think that jogging is the answer to man's long-sought prayer for fitness and good health. Editorials in respected medical journals have repeatedly made this point. As L. H. Nahum, M.D., former editor of *Connecticut Medicine*, pointed out, "The influence of work, exercise and stress on the cardiopulmonary system has not been adequately defined and in fact some of the data has been inadequate from which to form a clinical judgment." This opinion was reinforced by an editorial in the *Journal of the American Medical Association* (April 10, 1967) called "Exercise and Heart Disease": "There is justification for the viewpoint that the burden of proof still rests on those who state that increased physical activity will prevent, modify, or delay coronary heart disease. Moreover, if physical activity is indeed of value, the type and extent of beneficial activity is not now known." It's possible that in years to come the medical profession will discover that excessive exertion is detrimental rather than beneficial for the heart. So far it's all just speculation on what exercise holds for those who practice it. What will happen years later? Will such hearts be worn out prematurely?

It is true that, in the short run, exercise seems to improve the functions of the heart by increasing stroke volume, lowering cholesterol, increasing the vital capacity of the lungs, and promoting general fitness. But is all this fuss and energy expenditure in jogging worth the effort when we aren't certain whether such exercise is harmless?

For years I have contended that relaxation is better for hearts than overactivity, but many doctors, hyped on the need for strenuous exercise to "strengthen the heart," are distressed by my impertinent disbelief of their theory. When I ask them for proof that exercise prevents heart attacks and promotes good health, they fail to produce it.

I have never believed that throwing your skeleton and muscles around with abandon will help you achieve good health, and someone had to stand up and be counted. When I wrote *You Don't Have to Exercise* (Garden City, N.Y.: Doubleday & Company, 1942), I was called a nonconformist. Lately, I have again been warning of the dangers and ineffectiveness of extreme exertions, so it is not surprising that I've been labeled a medical maverick by some ardent joggers.

I do not bat an eye. Instead, I remind myself of the statement by Paul Williamson, M.D. who said, "We doctors have shared in the violent desire for conformism. We are as much alike as peas in a pod. If one of us dares to be a little different, he is censured and bedeviled until he is forced to conform. This is not a good thing for the medical profession. We need the independent thinker and the scoffer at custom just as we need the ultraconservative."

I do not consider myself a scoffer at my colleagues, but I admit that I do not admire their concerted rush to convert their patients into physically fit machines that can jog a few miles farther this week than they could the week before.

A study of current books on running and jogging does not reveal many instances in which doubts have been raised about the efficacy of exertions in promoting good health and fitness. Despite all that remains unknown about the effects of regular strenuous exercise, all such books seem to stress the unquestioned good that exercise will bring, and there's little allusion to potential dangers of intense exertion.

Many laymen also question the need for jogging, and this advice of a 75-year-old father to his "young" son is well taken:

Dear Son:
   Somehow it has gotten around that if you don't exercise you will die young; that a heart attack will shuffle you off prematurely. I suppose this is why you've lately taken to jogging every day. As I've always told you, the choice of your way of life is your own. I respect your decision. Nevertheless, if you recall our years together, my motto has been "moderation against immoderation in all things." Therefore, I hope you will be patient if I seem to repeat myself.

Exercise, to my mind, is fetishism. It has killed more people than it has helped. Yet, for years you have been adjuring me to take more exercise. But laziness hasn't prevented me from reaching a healthy 75 years of age; while you, my son, at 52 still need the calendar to prove that your way of life is good, too. (And for your sake, I hope it is).

As you know my exercise consists of walking moderately, and rubbing myself down vigorously with a towel after my morning shower. When I overeat or overdrink, I am quickly aware of it and take the necessary steps to eat less and drink less.

The point I'm trying to make is that no one should lightly tell a person he needs exercise to take off weight. If he has a potbelly, exercise may overstrain his heart and spell his doom. Exercise may hasten the inevitable. When I say exercise, I mean overstraining exertion such as too much jogging.

If one does not know his own body, and does not appreciate its limitations, then exercise is a hapless remedy. Incidentally, I agree with you that the body is a machine. It has to be used constantly; but neither overused nor abused by inertia. Let's agree that exercise is necessary, but only in smaller doses at the age of 52.

Love,
Dad

As I indicated previously, not all physicians agree that exercise is essential for your fitness and good health. Many eminent doctors, whom I'll quote later in this book, are trying to counteract such blanket advice. Exercise should not be prescribed offhandedly, but with serious consideration for the needs of each individual patient. It should be custom tailored.

I believe that misjudgments reach their peak when recent heart attack victims are advised to "go out and jog." That many have been carefully evaluated before such exertions is not entirely reassuring to anyone familiar with the gaps in medical knowledge.

And consider the vast number who jog without knowing their physical capabilities. Often, as I watch joggers, I try to guess which ones have recently had a physical checkup. I wonder how many rely on an examination they had years before and how many, young or old, have never had a complete cardiac checkup before straining and pulling to complete their daily jogging routine. I would guess that most people who jog are not the picture-book joggers you read about in the running manuals—that most are not running by formula and have not thoroughly investigated their cardiac status before engaging in stressful exertions.

HOW THE JOGGING REVOLUTION BEGAN

As I recall, the medical profession became excited about the need for exercise after a report in the British Medical Journal published in 1953 by a British physician, Dr. J. N. Morris, and his associates. They studied drivers and conductors of double-decker buses and motormen and guards of underground railways. About 30,000 men in these groups were between the ages of 35 and 60. After four years of observation the doctors reported that both the conductors and the guards had less coronary disease than the drivers and motormen, whose jobs required them to sit for more than the men in the other two groups. The researchers also found that government clerks who sat all day suffered more coronary attacks than postmen. They concluded that men in physically active jobs have a lower incidence of coronary heart disease in middle age than men in physically inactive jobs.

In December, 1958, Dr. Morris and Dr. Margaret Crawford issued a report based on pathological studies of 5000 men. About 1200 had died of coronary disease. They found less arterial involvement among "heavy workers than in light workers." "Physical activity in work," Morris and Crawford concluded, "is a protection against coronary heart disease. Men in physically active jobs have less coronary heart disease during middle age; what disease they have is less severe, and they develop it later than men in physically inactive jobs."

But then Morris and Crawford turned the light of truth on their own observations and tried to look at all sides of the problem. Many doctors have forgotten or were unaware of their real hesitancy about their findings: "It must be emphasized, however, that all over, the evidence on this problem is quite conflicting. In several studies, coronary heart disease has been found to be associated with physical activity/inactivity of occupation in the expected way. In as many, no relationship was demonstrated, or an equivocal or opposite one; and why this is so is still quite unclear."

How many of the high-spirited advocates of exercise who are trying to transform us into a nation of joggers are aware (or admit) this equivocation on the part of the oft-quoted British physicians? Studying the life-styles of hundreds of coronary patients in my own practice substantiated the conclusions of Dr. Morris and his associates. There is no clear connection between exercise or lack of exercise and coronary attacks.

Moreover, I have often wondered how many of the conductors suffered from hypertension and how many had diabetes? What were their family histories? How much exercise did conductors take after working hours? Think of how much tension motormen suffered while driving the buses through crowded streets. Was the increased heart attack rate due to lack of exercise or to something else?

COUNTERBALANCING STATISTICS

Yes, there are counterbalancing statistics. For example, in Norway and Sweden, the incidence of coronary disease is high among light and heavy workers alike. And in Japan, Italy, and South Africa, it is equally low among both sedentary and active workers.

Dr. Louis Katz and associates of Chicago stated that in the United States there was "a high prevalence and incidence of coronary disease in all sectors of the middle-aged male labor force, irrespective of nationality, socioeconomic status, income, occupation, physical activity or work, urban or rural residency."

As Arthur Blumenfeld noted in his book *Heart Attack: Are You a Candidate:* (PAUL S. ERIKSSON, Inc., New York 1964) "Dr. J. M. Chapman of Los Angeles has uncovered statistical evidence that the most active workers in the civil services in California have the same amount of coronary disease as those doing medium or light work."

Blumenfeld also pointed out that Dr. D. Spain's autopsy studies of 1960 showed that in every age group active and sedentary workers had the same amount of atherosclerosis.

Advocates of vigorous exercise often mention that jogging will lower cholesterol. The findings of Lawrence A. Golding, in 1962 director of the Exercise Physiology Laboratory at Ohio State University, are interesting on this point: "It isn't necessary to exercise vigorously as part of the [heart] prevention program. A moderate amount of exercise will be found sufficient to normalize blood cholesterol provided calories are watched and the diet fats are properly selected and consumed in moderation."

I have seen many fat joggers on the road. As they jog along, they have the mistaken belief that jogging will protect their hearts. In the opinion of Dr. A. M. Adelstein of the University of Manchester, "Another reason for the seemingly low protective effect of exercise [against heart disease] in the United States is the excessively rich diet. In communities where incidence of atherosclerotic heart disease is high, the causal (diet) factors tend to swamp any protective influence that may be exerted by exercise."

Medical theories change over the years. A few years from now do not be surprised to see a 180-degree change in the prevailing view. The experts of that day will be saying that the rested heart is the healthier heart and that such a heart will beat longer and more effectively than the exercised heart. When Dr. Raymond Pearl of Johns Hopkins said that death came soonest to the most active animals, he was undoubtedly thinking of the long-lived, lazy elephant, tortoise, and parrot.

CASE HISTORY: OLD ATHLETE AT 33

His wife was concerned about him, and at last George came in for a medical examination. His story went like this: "Once a week I play basketball with the boys. Not with my own children, but with fellows whose ages range between 19 and 23. As I'm 33, they call me the 'old man'.

"To try to prove that I'm not, I admit I overdo. I run and defend and attack as though my life depended on it. I know the reason. I never made the team at school. I keep trying to prove myself to myself. I guess I wonder if I have the stuff. Besides, I like a good workout.

"My wife tells me I'm overstraining myself. Frankly, when I get home I'm pooped. I'd like your opinion. Is such exercise harmful? After all I'm far from senile at age 33."

My advice to George was that he was out of his class. If one isn't a trained, professional athlete, ten years make quite a difference in one's ability to take the stress of exertion during competition.

Of course, George was not an old man at 33, but he wasn't young, either. Relatively speaking, his companions may be right in calling him "old man" on the basketball court. As one British cardiologist put it, "No arteries are normal after the age of 30," and what he was saying to people like George was this: Your arteries may be normal enough for the ordinary requirements of life, but not for the sustained stress of unusual exertion.

George's wife has good reason for being concerned. She had watched him running, shoving, being pushed, and fighting for breath as he subconsciously tried to convince the youngster in himself that the "old man" was just as fit as the rest of them. Men between 20 and 30 get coronary attacks, too. It's not common, but it's possible, and it happens. The armed services proved that.

I asked George if he had had a physical and an ECG before he took part in all that exertion. He hadn't, and I pointed out that that was the least he might have done to safeguard his health. Mind you, I was not against George's playing basketball for a workout, but he should have played it with other men his own age. He would have found that the pace didn't "poop" him so much. What's true for basketball is true for other sports, too. For example, tennis fans should play with those of their own age group. Otherwise, they may be piling up a lot of trouble in their hearts. Exercise will not impair the healthy heart, but too many middle-aged athletes simply guess that their heart is all right. This is one reason why so many get into needless trouble: they play guessing games with their hearts. Periodic checkups are cheap premiums to pay for survival.

George had listened attentively, but he was far from ready to accept that any of this had much application to him. "I had a great workout yesterday", he said. "None of the guys had the nerve to call me the old man. I was sinking baskets like a pro."

Complacently, he sat back as I took his history. I learned that his father had died of a heart attack at 42. An uncle had suffered a stroke at 48. His mother, though still alive at 55, was being treated for hypertension. Unquestionably, it was a poor family history.

Heredity was not on his side, and there were other negative factors: he smoked at least two packs of cigarettes daily; and he weighed at least twenty pounds above his estimated normal. Before examining him I said, "You know, I suppose, that you have at least two strikes against you already: poor heredity, and the combined habits of overeating, smoking, and overexerting."

George looked at me quizzically and flexing his arm and forearm muscles, said, "Feel them. Do they belong to someone who's going to topple over and die?"

I shook my head. "You appear to be in great shape except for your weight, but we'll know more after I've looked you over."

What demerits did I chalk up against our patient? First, apparently immature, he was unnaturally proud of his physique and athletic ability. Second, his blood pressure was slightly high, his poundage higher than normal, his cholesterol and triglyceride readings in the higher range of normal. On the positive side, his electrocardiogram was normal.

"Well, what do you think, doctor? Am I ready for the rocking chair?"

"I'm in favor of your workouts," I said, "but there are some exceptions and restrictions. One, stop trying to prove anything by playing with youngsters. Try to find basketballers your own age. Two, most patients your age do not require a yearly checkup, but with your family history and basketball exertions, you'd better come in twice a year for blood studies and electrocardiograms. Three, quit smoking. That's worse for you than behaving like a middle-aged athlete. Four, you are not yet ready for the rocking chair, but don't go around flexing your muscles at the age of 33. Leave that for preteens and teens. Stop trying to prove yourself."

I gave him that advice 25 years ago. Fortunately, this young man listened carefully and followed my suggestions. Today, at 58, he is a happy, contented husband, the father of three and grandfather of seven. His blood pressure, weight, ECGs, and blood studies are all within normal limits. He is a living example that poor heredity may be neutralized by a commonsense way of life. Our 33-year-old athlete had grown up. He had come to terms with overexercise, with bad habits, and with himself.

The other day I asked him, "Have you taken up jogging?"

I sensed his answer before he replied: "Who, me? What do I have to prove? I grew up way back when."

In *The Human Body* (Garden City, N.Y.: Doubleday & Company, 1927), Dr. Logan Clendening wrote, "Exercise and fresh air are supposed to be the sovereign augmenters of long life. I admit they make one feel better. That they promote longevity I seriously doubt. I instance two famous examples: Theodore Roosevelt and Walter Camp, both dying in their early sixties. On the other hand everyone knows a dozen octogenarians who have never taken a day's exercise in their lives."

2

JOGGING? FOR HORSES!

Suppose your doctor advises you to jog? If you are naturally lazy and a reluctant jogger, what should you do?

Perhaps the following imaginary conversation in a doctor's office will help you make up your mind:

DOCTOR: Do you jog?

YOU: No.

DOCTOR: I think you ought to. I'm a jogger myself.

YOU: Just what will jogging do for me?

DOCTOR: Help you keep fit. More important, it's good for your heart.

YOU: I thought you said my ticker is all right.

DOCTOR: It is. But where the heart's involved, I believe in trying to improve on perfection.

YOU: But I've read somewhere that jogging can be dangerous for a 45-year-old like myself.

DOCTOR: But I've just checked your heart. It's OK. You can go out and jog to your heart's content (if you don't mind the play on words.)

YOU: I'm not so sure. I had a friend who jogged every morning for two years. He dropped the day before yesterday, 10 minutes after returning from his usual morning jog.

DOCTOR: How old was he?

YOU: Only 38.

DOCTOR: That's about a one in a million shot at his age. Did he have a complete heart check recently?

YOU: His wife insisted that he have a stress test. His heart was apparently OK.

DOCTOR: But when you consider how good jogging is for you, I think it's silly to consider unlikely complications. Don't you?

YOU: I don't happen to be a gambler, doctor. Especially when my life's on the line. So do you mind if I beg off on this jogging bit?

DOCTOR: Not at all. It's your decision to make—even if I believe it's the wrong one.

YOU: Thanks, doctor. But I pass.

Negation should not be a fearsome experience in your doctor's office. Your doctor is not a God; not even a little god. If you ever suspect that his advice is questionable—at least as far as you are concerned—do not hesitate to question it.

It's evident that millions of joggers in the United States hate it. They have been coerced and cajoled into throwing their legs into daily exertions, like children who dislike music but just have to practice, or else!

My estimate is based on my observation that most human beings are lazy. It takes effort to jog. How many of the millions do it for the joy of it rather than for the hope of fitness? I think that at least 75 percent wish they had the guts and determination to stay in bed, rather than have to slip into shorts and sneakers to challenge the road.

Writing in the *Miami News* (July 14, 1978), Russel Baker, syndicated columnist for the N.Y. Times began his observations on exercise this way: "I don't jog. If this makes people who do jog feel smug about their muscle tone, so be it." Then he proceeded to confess to having been a jogger once and to knowing the dreariness and boredom it engendered. He promised himself that when he grew up he would never run again or jog. Then he became physically lazy, excluding almost all athletics. He considered that one of the few rewards of growing older was not having to "carry on" like that.

Occasionally, he'd have the urge to become vigorous, but he'd always be quick to assume the horizontal position again. He also has the quaint idea that he is actually helping his jogging friends by not jogging himself. Their contemplation of the "imminence of my demise," he surmises, helps them to endure.

Baker escapes the jogging epidemic because he is honest about his inclinations. If you are a jogger, I suggest this addition to your running equipment: a small hand mirror. Hold it up after you have been jogging for a while. Study your expression. Is it a happy face? Are your features relaxed? I doubt it. If you're a jogger and a masochist, you're having a splendid time. But if you're an innocent neophyte, talked into running a few days a week, it's likely you're having a bad time.

Observe your fellow joggers as they pass. Do you regularly see happy, smiling faces? Chances are they are serious and contorted.

I looked out my window the other day and saw a middle-aged man with a large paunch jogging by, a cigarette dangling from compressed lips. No doubt he was sure and determined that jogging was the antidote for two of his bad habits: smoking and overeating.

JOGGING CAN BE DANGEROUS

I consider such levels of overactivity potentially dangerous. Let me offer a sad example, a report I heard on the six o'clock news relating that a former officer of a heart institute had dropped dead at age 55 while jogging. According to his wife, he had recently suffered a heart attack. She believed that his doctor had advised—as many doctors still do—that he jog "to strengthen his heart."

An unusual tragedy? Not at all. It's likely that you have read or heard similar tragic reports in your own community. But let's turn to scientific observation. "Instantaneous and Sudden Deaths," was the title of an article by Meyer Friedman, M.D., and his associates at Mt. Zion Hospital and Medical Center, San Francisco (*Journal of the American Medical Association*, September 10, 1973). In studying the case histories of fifty-nine persons who died of coronary artery disease, these researchers found that more than one-half died during or immediately after physical exertion. Those who died within 30 seconds after the onset of any symptoms were listed as instant deaths; those in whom cardiac arrest occurred suddenly (a few minutes to 24 hours after the onset of symptoms or signs) were listed as sudden deaths. One of the subjects was a young man of 28 who had died instantly after completing twenty-seven successive chin-ups.

At the end of the study, the authors made the following comment:

> The close temporal relationship observed between severe or moderate physical activity and more than one half of the instantaneous death cases makes us question whether it is worth risking an instantaneous coronary death by indulging in an activity the possible benefit of which to the human coronary vasculature has yet to be proved.

They concluded their report with a statement that should be both revealing and disconcerting to those who feel no danger because they have been used to physical exertion since their younger days: "It also was disconcerting to find that many of our subjects who died during or immediately following their exertion had been well accustomed to the specific physical activity involved in this exertion."

I have observed similar tragic events in my own practice. Death is tragic wherever it occurs—in bed, for example. But it is ironic and especially mournful when it strikes down a jogger in quest of strengthening his heart. It is a mortal insult to the innocent!

What bothered me in reading several books on running and jogging was that the advocates of jogging seldom adequately stress the dangers of overexertion. And the innocents, intent on physical fitness, are unaware of potential threats to their health. Here are some additional reports that should help to neutralize the rash promises for the benefits of jogging and other stressful overexertions.

In his book *Diseases of the Heart* (W. B. Saunders, Philadelphia, 1956), Charles K. Friedberg, M.D., wrote that the patient often denies any unusual physical effort prior to the heart attack. However, questioning relatives and friends of heart attack victims, he found that there was usually some extraordinary activity that might have had a hand in the attack. These factors might have been responsible for the coronary attack hours, days, or even weeks before the appearance of symptoms.

Dr. Friedberg also noted similar findings by other heart

specialists. C. Smith, M.D., and his associates, for example, found that physical exertion was associated with the heart attack in thirty-two of fifty-three cases of coronary occusion. Dr.'s A. J. French and W. Dock found that twenty-six, or more than 30 percent, of the eighty fatal attacks of coronary disease that they studied occurred within one to several hours after vigorous exercise—lifting a heavy trunk, pushing a stalled car, rowing, taking a long uphill hike, or any unusual exercise performed when the patient was unduly fatigued or after little sleep.

Nevertheless, some few prominent physicians, addicted to physical exertion themselves, have led the way in promulgating the theory that "daily exercise is essential for good health." And unfortunately, this theory of overexertion has been accepted by many in the medical profession, in sheeplike credulity.

There are others, like myself, who disagree. When asked about jogging, Assistant Clinical Professor of Medicine at the University of California, James E. Anhalt, Sr., M.D., said, "I've never been much of a jogging enthusiast. If patients ask about jogging, I tell them to walk briskly." Dr. Herbert N. Hultgren, Professor of Medicine at Stanford University said, "I think there's an overemphasis on jogging. Everyone feels the only way to exercise is to jog."

I do not believe that you should give up exercise. Nor do I recommend that you live like an amoeba or like a semi-invalid imprisoned in your rocking chair. But why agonize to attain fitness? Why suffer? What does jogging offer that other exertion doesn't? Later in this book I will offer many ways to become fit without having to endure muscle revolt.

Will jogging prevent you from having a heart attack? Will it add years to your life? I do not believe so. Although moderate jogging may occasionally promote fitness, it does not guarantee health or longevity. You may be healthy and still not be fit. Likewise, you may be fit enough to jog and still be sick. One does not follow the other as B does A.

Exercise is not a "poison," nevertheless years of observing patients as a cardiologist and an internist has convinced me that jogging is natural exertion for horses but not for people.

Promises. Promises. That's all you've been hearing and reading lately. Please do not believe that jogging strengthens your heart and prolongs life. Medical experts agree there is no valid proof that this is so for exerters. Nor does jogging surely lower your blood pressure or relieve anxiety, depression, or the scores of other types of emotional and physical distress.

Although I agree that jogging may temporarily increase cardiac efficiency, remember this warning: unnatural strains and exertions may produce a sudden heart irregularity (ventricular fibrillation) that results in the sudden cessation of heartbeats, which is often a euphemistic way of describing a fatal heart attack.

PREDICTION

I renew a prediction I've often made: it won't be long before the jogging mania withers and dies. It is a passing fad, and the sooner it passes, the better. In a few years you will see few if any joggers plodding along the highways and byroads. Joggers will become an extinct species. At last doctors and their patients will have realized that jogging is an unnecessary, ridiculous, and exaggerated form of physical exertion for attaining physical fitness.

As I show later in this book, there are more responsible and sensible ways to stay healthy and keep your heart strong, to strive for good health, fitness, and longevity. The list has its basis in common sense and moderation:

Exercising moderately
Not smoking
Drinking in moderation (if at all)
Not overeating (to control obesity, cholesterol, and triglyceride abnormalities)
Learning how to control excessive stress and tension
Discovering and treating diabetes and hypertension early
Practicing simple exercises to strengthen your diaphragm
Learning how to walk
Knowing how to take naps

If you follow these suggestions, and others I'll tell you about later, you will have no need to exercise frantically to put the icing on the cake of fitness and good health.

Many doctors are slowly coming around to the theory that jogging is potentially harmful and not the specific answer on how to spare your heart and arteries.

For example, an interview printed in the *Miami Herald* (June 16, 1977), recorded the observations of a former officer of the Dade County Medical Society in Florida:

I am not totally convinced that jogging is worth what people have said. There is more and more [medical] literature to show that strenuous physical exercise, such as this, doesn't really add all that to a person's lifespan. I think good rapid walking, which is not strenuous and not difficult, is one of the best forms of exercise available.

Consider also the warning by Henry I. Russek, M.D., of New York, in the Journal, *Diseases of the Chest:* "The growing attachment of the medical profession [to the belief] that exercise heads the lists of requirements for a healthy heart often leads to misjudgment in the treatment of people with heart disease."

Examples of such misjudgments are known to most physicians.

An anxious wife of an insurance company executive in Connecticut lived in fear every time her husband went out jogging. He had suffered a heart attack only a few months previously, but his doctor prescribed jogging to "strengthen his heart muscle." He died at his desk one hour after he had quit jogging for the day. She lived in guilt for many years because she hadn't tried hard enough to convince him to give up his jogging.

The usual reassurance given is that some heart patients have run marathon races without dropping dead. If you insist on jogging be certain that you have been carefully evaluated before running any unnecessary risks.

A newspaper editor writing on jogging made some pertinent

observations often revealed in medical literature. Formerly a jogger himself, he became distressed when he learned that medical findings indicated enzymes similar to those found in tests of heart attack patients often appear in blood tests of joggers. In other words, he postulated that runners are sometimes afflicted by the very thing they run against. Indecisive about continuing to jog, he sought the advice of a doctor-friend who was an inveterate jogger and who convinced him to resume the exercise. However, the newspaper editor reported that one day the doctor "was out jogging vigorously, came in, and fell on his face. He never got up. I quit."

The editor concluded that civilian exercise should not be regimented. That, as individuals, we can overdo it: "The word is moderation."

If you are physically lazy, stay physically lazy. Don't feel it is necessary to follow the crowd of physical activists. Be content to relax without any twinges of conscience as you watch your friends jog by your hammock with religious fervor. Don't be influenced by the jogger who looks down upon you as his lazy neighbor. Like the recently converted smoker who is proud of his will in overcoming the tobacco habit, the jogger is not happy and fulfilled unless he converts you.

As you sit or lie back in comfort, say to yourself, "Does this jogger want to go running all over the place as if it's the answer to existence? Let him, if he enjoys it—although he doesn't seem to. As for me, I feel better lying around and recharging my battery by relaxing. Certainly, not by jogging."

THE NEW PSYCHIATRY

An almost unbelievable piece in *Time* magazine (July 24, 1978) reported that for five years a California psychiatrist has practiced psychotherapy while jogging along with his patients. He believes that jogging is a form of therapy and claims it is successful as a treatment for depression, drug addiction, and schizophrenia. He considers jogging a new, powerful way of reaching the unconscious. Another enthusiastic doctor says he plans to start a Jungian talk-and-jog therapy with neurotic patients, charging $75 an hour!

Doesn't it make more sense, however, to listen to doctors who, joggers themselves, are reserving judgment on the running "cure"? For example, psychiatrist Jerome Katz of the Menninger Foundation in the *Time* article cautions that "the enthusiastic claims of instant cures of depression have to be evaluated with a great deal of salt." In that same *Time* article, Clinton Cox, a reporter for the *New York Daily News* offered the real secret of the jogging "cure": "It's almost impossible to worry about your job or other such mundane pursuits when your body is in total agony."

James Bacon, in his book *Made in Hollywood* (Contemporary Books, Chicago, 1977) commented on Cary Grant's formula for fitness. Many girls prefer Cary Grant at 73 to younger stars. The reason is that Cary looks fit at that age. Yet his secret of youthfulness is not a secret at all; it was all so simple. "I really don't do a thing except relax and take things easy," said Cary. "I am constantly amazed to read that I distill vegetable juices, swim sixty laps daily as if I were training to swim the English Channel, and that I spend six hours a day in the gym working out.

"I don't do anything to keep fit. I get all the exercise I need just breathing in and out. And at my age, even that gets a bit exhausting."

Years ago, I heard that Chancellor Robert Hutchins of the University of Chicago was responsible for the famous saying "Whenever I feel like exercising I lie down until the feeling passes," so I asked permission to quote him in my book *You Don't Have to Exercise*. Dr. Hutchins replied he would gladly give consent, except that he wasn't the saying's author. But he added that he wished he had said it!

Cary Grant. Dr. Hutchins. What better examples of blessed constitutional inertia?

3
JOGGITIS: AN AMERICAN EPIDEMIC

According to a Gallup Poll in 1977, 47 percent of Americans participated in some kind of daily exercise. That's about twice the number recorded in 1961. Of the exercisers, about half are joggers. The New York Road Runner's Club, in two years, has tripled its membership to 6,000. Also according to a Gallup Poll, as related by John Van Doorn in *New York Magazine* (May 29, 1978), joggers are the "upscale" people, the college educated, those in upper and upper-middle income brackets, professionals, business people, the general run of white collar workers. Not exclusively, by any means, but they began it all. Gallup notes that "many behavioral and attitudinal trends in America follow the trickle-down process—that is, they are taken up by the affluent and higher-educated groups and are later picked up by others—and the case of exercise appears to be no different."

Doesn't it seem incredible that any doctor should have the temerity to stand up in full view of his peers to say that jogging is for horses, not for humans? Yet, I do not consider that it takes guts to invite condemnation by those who have become infected with the jogging bug—especially when they are guilty of spreading the infection to their patients. Unquestionably, jogging has become a raging epidemic. Millions suffer from it. When I predicted that within a few years you will rarely see even a lone jogger beating his legs against city pavement or country road, many enthusiastic joggers responded in dismay.

In 1977, for example, I received a kindly letter of disagreement from a prominent member and executive of the National Jogging Association; Richard L. Bohannon, M.D., President. He said, in effect, that there are 8 million joggers in the United States, and he smiled at my quaint idea that only horses should enjoy the benefits of jogging. He left to the future my prediction that jogging will soon disappear from the scene and observed that the main point of his association's disagreement with me is my "contention that fitness can be achieved and maintained without serious effort." He believes that no one enhances his or her fitness (oxygen consumption capacity) without perspiration. . . . "Please accept our congratulations on your positive recommendations for fitness. We concur wholeheartedly! If we could get you to bear down a little more on the value of a little perspiration, you'd see more smiling joggers. . . ."

I replied that medical theories change. Who is to say that in a decade or two most cardiologists will not agree that the way to save heartbeats for the long race is to be miserly and conserve them? We should all be open minded. I further told him that what disturbed me was that so many millions of this vast jogging fraternity had never had a comprehensive heart checkup. Newspaper stories and medical reports in our own medical journals tell of the unfortunate fatalities.

About the same time I received this letter, another came from the office of Mr. V. L. Nicholson, Director of Information, the President's Council On Physical Fitness and Sports. The correspondent for the council took issue with what he called "your recent diatribe on jogging." He was referring to my column which appeared in the *Washington Star* on June 28, 1977. His letter of disagreement concluded on an amusing note in reply to my statement that joggers rarely smile while working out: "So most joggers don't look happy? Well, Toscanini frequently frowned while he worked, Makarova usually looks solemn when she dances, and I am told that Michelangelo did not always wear a grin to the Sistine Chapel. The poor devils probably didn't (or don't) enjoy their work."

My reaction to overexercise is not new. My motive is not purposely to get out of step with current medical opinion. In the 1940s, I published You Don't Have to Exercise and about twenty years later another called How to Be Lazy, Healthy and Fit (New York: Funk & Wagnalls Company, 1968). I have also published articles on exercise in *Reader's Digest* and in the old *Saturday Evening Post*, reiterating my belief that Americans periodically go beserk in search of physical fitness. As they're doing now! My antipathy to overexertion has not abated.

I'm certainly more than a nonconformist. Many call me a medical maverick. The difference is that whereas the former refuses to lie down and be branded with the rest of the sheep, the latter not only refuses to lie down, but fights to jump up and proclaim his beliefs to the world, contrary though they may be to the majority opinion.

I consider joggers to have a masochistic streak and the doctors and others who advise them to jog to be sadistic. In addition, I consider that people "tuned in" on body fitness are narcissistic. There's something about a jogger that turns me off. Is it a certain piety of self-sacrifice? Is it a smugness and sense of superiority? Is it an unfounded pride of accomplishment?

For me, two-legged jogging is a cruel joke—and sometimes a tragedy. Whenever I look upon the suffering faces of joggers, I wonder what is the real, underlying motive. To join a cause? Religious fervor? Vanity? To save the heart? To beat off the threat of old age? The quest for longevity?

According to Dr. Richard Schwartz, "It's taken us years to convince Type As that they should get out of competitive sports. Now instead of competing against somebody in tennis or racquetball, they're competing with themselves over how many miles they can run and are often comparing their performances with their associates.

Jules Pfeiffer in one of his cartoon strips depicts a jogger who begins only because his doctor has prescribed it for his health. His endurance increases, and at last he is not jogging for competition any more. "I jog for glory!" he says.

In *The Complete Runner*, by Editors of *Runner's World* (World

Publications, 1974), you will find this description of the dedicated jogger:

"Running is a self-centered sport with high demands on time, energy and attention. When it gets to be like a second job or a mistress, family stresses often show up—in marriage and mileage not mixing well.". . . According to Dr. Bruce Ogilvie, runners are "self-battling, inward-looking loners. Running is a self-imposed loneliness."—In general, runners want to be apart, not together; to escape, not join; to feel unique, not alike; to find self, not company."

Here is Brenda Woods writing about jogging in a New York News Service article:

Boredom has always been the eighth deadly sin, a malady none of us wants to come down with. But sometimes, just trying too hard not to be a bore can make you the worst one of all. . . .

Jogging is almost like the weather lately. A lot of people never do much about it, but they do talk about it a lot. Please, we don't mind if you do it, but we do mind hearing about it, reading about it and, above all, looking at your latest jogging outfit.

PROMISES

At times I wonder why I react to jogging with such distaste. But I know. I'm upset by the promises, promises, promises that are made by its proponents. Whoever the author on jogging and its benefits, you are likely to read about the benefits of jogging but find few specific warnings about the potential dangers of overexertion except the vague one "better have an examination."

For example, in the July 1978 *Reader's Digest* there was an article "Run Your Way to Happiness," written by James F. Fixx. A *Reader's Digest* editor heads up the article this way: "Why have millions of Americans become obsessed with running? More than fitness is involved, says the author of the year's surprise best-seller [The Complete Book of Running]. Runners have discovered a source of power and joy that the sedentary can't imagine."

The article by Fixx is condensed from the author's book *The Complete Book of Running*, Random House, N.Y.C. 1977. He quotes one runner who runs six miles four to five times a week as saying, "A good run makes you feel sort of holy." Others Fixx quotes say that it relieves anxiety, and that by increasing one's self-esteem and independence," it is the answer to depression.

Fixx also recounts the story of a victim of asthma who said that before he took up running, "Every gasp was terrible. I couldn't think about anything else." "Then," says Fixx, "he took up running. Although he is careful not to claim that running cured his asthma, he does say that it has been a principal factor in causing the attacks to stop."

For those who would prefer a more scientific account of the effects of jogging on asthma the *New England Journal of Medicine* (May 4, 1978) contained a revealing account by Stanley Hoyt Block, M.D.:

"A 34-year-old physician, in excellent health, started jogging during December. He had no history of wheezing, shortness of breath or asthma.—Two minutes after completing his first day of jogging, he experienced acute wheezing—He continued to jog each day for the next week and he experienced the same exercise-induced asthma.—He discontinued the jogging; however, the episodes of wheezing continued daily for three weeks. After three weeks without jogging the spontaneous non-exercise-induced wheezing stopped. . . . About a month later, the doctor started jogging again; again, exercise-induced asthma developed after each run. . . . He finally gave up jogging permanently and within three weeks all wheezing disappeared, never to recur.—This patient demonstrates a very common side effect of jogging—namely, exercise-induced asthma. . . .

The confessions of a man who has been running for twenty-five years give some insight into the psychological reasons why one would run. This jogger sustained injury during a foot race. He tried short rests, taping, heat, cold, heelcups, sponge rubber pads, cortisone, and scores of different pairs of shoes. Nothing helped until he took the advice of a podiatrist to rest. He was soon running again, "But what of these past two weeks of rest?" he asks himself.

What does a seventy-mile-a-week runner do when suddenly forced to quit cold turkey on a 25-year-old habit? He freaks out, right? He climbs the walls and drives everybody around him crazy.

Good guess, and true for lots of guys I know, but for me? Wrong! It has been nice not having to run every day. No plodding through the stifling heat and humidity. No nagging conscience all day until I get my run in. No worry about staying up to watch "Saturday Night Live" knowing I had a brutal twelve-mile run waiting for me at 6:30 the next morning. [Would you say he loves to run or hates it? Read on.]

Don't get me wrong. I really do like to run and I'll be glad when I can really get back to it. It's hard to describe how much I look forward to running without pain, how great it will be when my right foot feels the same as my left and the only pain I have to contend with is that resulting from hard effort. [Loves it?]

But for now, I can't say I've missed the heavy burden that serious training entails. [Hates it?]

Admittedly, running is drudgery at times, but there is real pleasure in doing something difficult and staying with it. [Twenty-five years of pain, drudgery, and pleasure?]

Says one concerned wife: "My husband is killing himself. He was a great athlete at school. Now that he's 42 he still thinks he's great. He hasn't much time for tennis or golf so he has taken up running. He works hard all day, yet insists on running five to ten miles when he comes home from work. He comes in the back door to shed his running pants and sneakers and heads for the shower. He looks exhausted and like death itself. What can I do to save him?"

I may be helpful if he takes the time to read this book. But experience tells me that exercise addiction is difficult to cure. A heart attack or some other physical disability is more certain to turn the overexerciser into a rational human being.

Her husband is not alone. Observe the taut, strained faces of many of these misguided middle-aged athletes. They clearly indicate they are not having fun, but doing it only because "exercise is good for you."

Overestimating your physical capabilities is the danger in an overzealous search for physical fitness. People, doctors included, often forget that overexercise can destroy the whole organism. It is especially dangerous to try to make up for fifty weeks of inactivity by two weeks of overactivity while on vacation. This just invites a heart attack.

Overestimating your physical capabilities in trying to disprove the limitations set by your calendar age is another special danger. How many times have we heard of a 65-year-old who suffered a heart attack while helping his children move something heavy. "Dad, take it easy. We don't need your help". But Dad insists. "You're trying to make an old codger out of me." And the chest pains come and wash away his helpfulness and turn it into helplessness.

IS YOUR HEART HEALTHY?

Remember that your heart and blood vessels are your pump and inner tubing. However sound you think you are, you can depend on it that if you are over 30 the tubing has had some microscopic punctures and slow leaks silently patched by mother nature. Commonsense dictates avoiding excessive speeds to prevent a sudden blowout.

Unfortunately, you may not be willing to accept restrictions. You think it is a premature surrender to age. You are like the overactive character in Tennessee William's Cat on a Hot Tin Roof" who says: "People like to do what they used to do even after they've stopped being able to do it."

When have you had your last physical checkup? It is true that strenuous exertion will not strain the healthy heart. But are you certain your heart's healthy? Do you know its capacity for exertion? Not forgetting the pump, how are your arteries?

You may be related to cave men and women, but you aren't living in a cave today. Your ancestors had to be physically fit from the neck down to survive. On the contrary, you have to be fit from your Adam's apple up to live.

When asked how much exercise an office worker needs to keep fit,

Dr. Robert Darling said, "Fit for what?—You're physically fit if your body can get you through your day's work.—As for exercise itself, it's been the subject of a lot of nonsense."

Alden H. Syper reaches deep down into the psychological explanation of overexertion when he says, "It seems there is a far greater need in this nation and in the world than the ability to run a mile, which qualifies a man to run another, or to be able to do twenty pushups, which fits a man to do twenty more tomorrow."

In the 1940s, Thomas Costain, editor and historical novelist, asked me to write a book for Doubleday and Company. He said, "If you haven't any preference, how about one on exercise?" I agreed and wrote the book I have mentioned previously, *You Don't Have to Exercise*.

It was my first book for Doubleday. Not until years later did I learn why he was so interested in the subject of exercise. When he was in his seventies, he confessed that he favored a relaxed way of life and was allergic to physical exertion. Yet, in spite of this attitude, he remained a tall, fit, well-built figure of a man.

Nonexercisers are legion. But they don't proclaim about the benefits of leisure as the exercisers do about the benefits of physical exertion. Instead, they go quietly about their way.

MEDICAL SUPERVISION

Admittedly, exercises should be medically supervised. But how many, I ask, of the millions who jog, who do pushups or engage in other activities are ever under medical supervision? And how many, once having undertaken an exercise program, persevere daily month after month? Even Dr. Kenneth Cooper, author of *Aerobics,* Bantam Books, N.Y.C. 1972 warns that "people are going at it too hard and too fast, not following the guidelines—and they are killing themselves."

I am happy to read that Dr. Cooper's credo about medical examinations before jogging is this:

• Younger than 30 years: medical history and physical examination within the preceding year. That applies even to high school athletes.

• From 30 to 35: history and resting electrocardiogram within six months.

• 35 and older: resting and stress ECG within three months. ("I am not that emphatic about this up to 40," Cooper said, "but we are seeing a lot of heart disease between 35 and 40.")

• Nobody should push himself beyond the point that it takes more than ten minutes to recover to a heartbeat of one hundred beats a minute or less, Cooper said.

But I ask you for a candid reply. How many of the millions of joggers do you think follow the precepts put down by Cooper and the suggestions by doctors all over to be sure to have physical checkups before participating in a jogging program?

Watch the joggers on the road. For a moment forget about those younger joggers and gaze upon those apparently older than 35. How many have had stress electrocardiogram tests? How many can afford to pay $150 or more for the tests? How many take the time? How many repeat the tests after they have been jogging six months or longer? Forget for the moment that there aren't enough stress test laboratories or clinics, in doctors' offices or elsewhere, to take care of the 8 million fitness enthusiasts the National Joggers Association claims are jogging. That, of course, is one statistic that leaves me incredulous: 8 million joggers! How did anyone arrive at that figure? Even with the thousands that show up to run marathon races, I can't conceive that the few struggling joggers one sees here and there, add up to millions.)

Your candid opinion about how many of the supposed 8 million joggers have had even one stress test? Few. Very few. So what is the good of all these warnings by jogging enthusiasts that jogging is safe because people have their medical checkups to insure their hearts "can take it."

If, in spite of what I have been saying, you decide on an exercise program for physical fitness to "save your heart," be sure to have a cardiologist test your aerobic capacity on a treadmill or bicycle ergometer. He will specify your Critical Heart Rate, which is the pulse rate at which ECG changes may take place or anginal symptoms become evident.

He will teach you how to estimate your "target rate" (maximal predicted heart rate for your age). In teenagers, for example, the target rate is 220 beats per minute during exercise. You calculate your own rate by subtracting your age from 220. To be on the safe side, some use the 200 figure.

For example, if you are 60 years old, 200 minus 60 equals 140. If he wants you to use only 60 percent during convalescence, your target pulse will be 140 times .6 or 84 beats per minute. As you progress in fitness he will allow you to increase your target rate during exercise. As you can see, your pulse rate during exertion is the magical key that opens the door to successful rehabilitation after a heart attack.

THE STRESS TEST

Suppose you decide to have a stress test? What can you expect? I could explain in cold, measured, scientific terms how your heart would be monitored by radiotelemetry or a direct-wire system. But that would not describe the subjective sensations the patient undergoes while in the small room, on the treadmill, constantly under observation by a doctor and nurse.

Instead, I'll offer the reactions of columnist Charles Whited, who graphically described his own sensations in the Miami Herald on June 18, 1978. In part, he wrote: "It was a brisk walk, uphill. By stages, the treadmill beneath my feet shifted to higher speeds, and steeper slopes. After nine minutes, I was doing 3.4 miles per hour on a 14 per cent grade.

"I sweated and puffed. My leg muscles felt the strain. My bare chest and sides bristled with electrodes and wires. A junction box rode my midsection. Before me, an electronic console flashed data.

" 'How are you feeling?' It was my cardiologist, a woman doctor, speaking.

"Just (puff, puff) fine." The treadmill shifted to Stage 4. My legs pumped faster. Digital readouts flicked on the console: heartbeat 165, speed 4.2 miles per hour, grade 16 per cent.

"—I was wearing down. The inexhaustible electronic console continued to flash digital data. The heartbeat reached 167, or 95 per cent of my capacity. The cardiologist took my blood pressure for the fourth time. Now, at peak, it was 230 over 80. A trifle high, but still in the normal range. I gasped: 'That's enough.'

"The treadmill slowed, gradually it stopped. I stepped off, dripping sweat. My recovery was rapid, the heartbeat back to nearly normal after six minutes. There were no apparent irregularities. I would be able to run as far as I liked, but should keep my heartbeat, by occasional pulse checks, in the 140 to 150 range.

"The cardiologist was pleased. 'I see no risk', she said, 'in your continued running. Just don't get hit by a truck.'

This is truly a heartening description of a stress test. But I'm afraid I'll have to stick a pin into her balloon of complacency. Although stress tests are important, and often give early indication of trouble that was unsuspected, they are not infallible. Playing safe after a normal test, perhaps we doctors should say "I see less risk" rather than "I see no risk."

At the age of 49, Charles Whited decided to take a stress test because "Jogger health nuts like me, however, are dropping dead in their jogging shoes, at midstride—. Dade County (Miami) can count half a dozen dead joggers in a year. All of heart attacks."

That was his motivation. Undoubtedly, his column convinced many other joggers to take similar precaution.

In the *Internist Reporter* (February 1976), there appeared an article entitled "Heart Specialists Call Unsupervised Exercise 'Suicide'."

San Francisco: Exercise can be an invitation to suicide for the unsupervised patient, two cardiologists warned here recently.

Dr. Ezra Amsterdam of the University of California, told the American College of Cardiology, that no asymptomatic patient over 35 should exercise before having a thorough physical examination including a maximum exercise stress test.

If the examination shows any evidence of coronary disease, the patient "should only exercise with trained personnel available," he said.

Otherwise, walking should be the limit for this patient. He should be taught to take his own pulse and "keep 35 to 40 heart beats away from ischemia," he said.

Dr. Amsterdam was joined in his warnings on exercise by Dr. Meyer Friedman of Mount Zion Hospital and Medical Center here, who said he was "sick and tired of the number of people dropping dead from jogging. The news is just not getting around."

Dr. Friedman said he believes that in people with known heart disease, jogging unsupervised is a "very real risk," with one death reported for every five to six thousand hours of exercise.

"Treadmill tests don't show ischemia in half of those who have it," he observed and *"if I had to write my book again, I would not give clearance to anyone jogging if he had a normal treadmill. With a normal angiogram, I would say yes."*

Killjoy: I'll accept the label if you balance it against the ultimate danger. What I want to stress is that I do not accept the statement "I see no risk" when a heart is put through the nth degree of labor. Treadmill tests for heart disease may not be as accurate as was once thought. It is an essential part of a complete heart checkup to take an electrocardiogram while the heart is undergoing stress, but *Medical Letter*, a newsletter for physicians, agrees with Dr. Friedman that the stress test isn't 100 percent reliable. One study found that 30 to 50 percent of the men who had a positive stress test displayed no other symptoms or signs and were actually free of heart disease. Erroneous treadmill test results can thus lead to psychological problems and unnecessary physical restrictions. The article in *Medical Letter* reported that it's also possible for stress tests to miss underlying heart disease, leading "some people to dangerously overestimate their capacity for exercise."

Whenever I read such warnings, I inevitably turn back to what Dr. Raymond Pearl of John Hopkins wrote: "The evidence also tends to show that persons who avoid too strenuous exercise after 40, and do not engage in heavy musuclar labor, have a much better chance of long life than the misguided chap who overtaxes his middle-aged boilers with a freshman head of steam."

If you are over 35 and have had a stress test, you have at least taken reasonable precautions that are likely—but not guaranteed—to prevent sudden the cardiac failure known as a heart attack. But don't let anyone talk you into taking isometric exercises—one set of muscles pushing against another. Although this type of exercise may help muscle development, it causes abnormal tensions that raise the blood pressure and are detrimental to the heart. Aerobic exercise is more natural, producing motion and less tension.

Neither should you undertake an exercise program if you have any of the following conditions: congenital heart disease; rheumatic heart disease; very high blood pressure, uncontrollable by medication; angina pectoris which seems to be getting worse (unstable angina); possible preinfarction angina; unexplainable persistent heart skips; or ventricular aneurysm (weakening of the wall of the heart.)

I recently read a question put out by an ardent exerciser and the answer given by the physician. For evident reasons, I will not reveal names, or even initials. Read carefully, and decide what you would suggest.

Dear Doctor:
    Are 1000 sit-ups every morning OK for me? I'm 57, and after six months of graduating from 25 to 50 to 1000 and more, I can now do 1000 and sometimes 1200 in an easy forty-five minutes.
    I feel, act and perform as well as any teenager, I think. Since I've reached my goal of trimming my waistline and have reduced from 165 to 140, I'm going by the rule that the best thing about exercise is don't stop. Am I right? Incidentally, after sit-ups and a shower, I have three or four sixteen-ounce beers and a big breakfast, then I'm off to work. Am I overdoing anything?

Dear Exerciser:
    You might be overdoing it a bit on the beer, but that's your business. As for the sit-ups, I salute your stamina and can only affirm what you already know, that all that activity is good for

cardiovascular fitness and will keep your stomach and heart strong and able. You're not doing much for your legs or other muscle groups, however, and I'd suggest you branch out into a more balanced program. How about 10,000 leg lifts?

When masochist and sadist meet, your guess about the outcome is as good as mine! It's evident that jogging is not the only method man has devised to throw his torso and muscles around.

I disagree with doctors who routinely prescribe exercise programs for patients who have suffered a myocardial infarction three months earlier. I believe that most patients cannot be trusted to follow explicitly the doctor's directions. They either overdo or underdo, and in the former case, they endanger themselves by trying to make up for lost time.

If you have had a heart attack, overexertion is less conducive to overall fitness than commonsense, unstudied exertions; a philosophy of relaxation and freedom from unnecessary tensions; proper weight and blood pressure control; and a resolve not to smoke or overdrink.

Here are some interesting conclusions offered by Dr. Howard R. Pyfer after he had studied the effects of exercise training therapy among 792 patients in a Seattle program and at other West Coast facilities:

- Coronary heart disease patients exercise at risk. Several months of regular training does not guarantee protection.
- Arrest [heart stoppage] cannot be predicted on the basis of age, exercise tolerance test findings, type of duration of exercise.
- Training provides positive physiological and psychological benefits in the overall rehabilitation process.

Dr. Pyfer reported that two patients experienced cardiac arrest while jogging, five while walking after jogging, four while standing after jogging, one while walking prior to jogging, and two during calisthenics. "All were revived by electrical defibrillation without residual cardiac or brain damage." But Dr. Pyfer also reported that "thirty-four other patients died when they experienced cardiac arrest outside of the facilities where resuscitation equipment and personnel are at hand."

Ask yourself how many of the millions of joggers and other overexerters exercise within reach of "resuscitation equipment and personnel"? This includes you. There lies the danger. And how many, including you, have recently had a comprehensive heart checkup? Feeling well is no guarantee of being well. One estimate is that one out of four persons with coronary heart disease doesn't know he or she has it. Then consider how many jog and overexert with the equivalent of dynamite in their back pockets.

As an internist and cardiologist I am aware of the benefits exercise can bring to your heart. But I also am aware of the potential dangers of overexercise, especially in those who do not suspect that their circulation lacks the efficiency to withstand the exertions.

For example, at the age of 45 Joe Doakes, recently examined and pronounced fit, might safely play handball a few times weekly. But suppose he does not believe in the need for periodic physical checkups and, as most others do, just guesses that his heart is all right? He might easily kill himself one day. He would be healthier and more fit by taking a daily nap to relax, than by exerting in the gym or on the road without true knowledge of his heart's capacity.

Joggers say that you can save heart beats in the end because the heart beats more slowly after exercise training. Maybe so, but there's danger that you may drop dead before reaching the bank to deposit those extra beats. So better not gamble.

This, then, is the crux of my belief that overexercise by jogging can threaten health and life: without constant supervision, most people are not fit enough to undergo exertions that call on the heart's reserves. Don't plunge into the exercise pool without even knowing how to swim, without knowing if your heart can withstand extreme exertions.

Don't be one of the millions of joggers who have not had a heart evaluation. And even though your doctor says "there's absolutely nothing to worry about, your heart's fine," play it safe by erring on the side of not jogging too hard or too long. Be thankful that you have a good heart, and try to keep it that way as long as you can. It can be done—as I'll show later—without a trying exercise regime.

To emphasize a point, sometimes you have to repeat it ad nauseum. So I'll not excuse myself by saying again that overexertion has killed many innocent men. I recall one 36-year-old attorney who prided himself on his physical fitness. He played hard at tennis, squash, and body-building exercises, and then he took up jogging. Like the man with the cough who swallowed the entire bottle of medicine at once so he would quickly feel better, our young barrister was not content with jogging a mile or two a day. He didn't rest easy until he jogged an average of ten miles every day. He wanted instant fitness. His wife kept asking him to have a checkup.

"I've had one," he said. But that was on his thirtieth birthday. What had happened during the ensuing six years? He could only guess that his heart was all right. "Besides", he said, "I'm too young to have a heart attack."

One Sunday morning the guessing game ended. A sudden heart attack while jogging laid him low. Fortunately, he survived, but he jogs no more. Happy endings aren't the rule for people who overexert, guessing that their heart is strong enough to endure all-out exertion. If you are a jogger, you can't afford to guess your heart is all right.

Although a recent visit to a doctor is no guarantee that you are not in danger, it's less likely that you'll be a victim. I can't accept, however, the blanket advice of jogging proponents: "Have a checkup before you jog." Having said that, they feel their consciences are clear. "We've warned them, haven't we?"

Ask them what percentage of joggers really know the condition of their hearts. Surely not 100 percent, nor 80 percent, nor even 50 percent. My guess is that not more than 10 percent of active joggers have had a heart checkup within six months. And what type of heart examination? Surely, all do not have complicated and expensive stress tests.

I'll leave the answer to you. Most joggers run at their own risk. And too many, like our attorney, think they are too young to have a heart attack. Physiological age, not calendar arithmetic is what matters.

A sad incident reported in the press recently is by no means unusual. A 34-year-old man died while jogging near his home. The police said he was wearing only blue tennis shoes, white shorts, and a gold chain and charm. An officer found him lying on a grassy knoll just off the street. The temperature was 85 on a humid day.

It is ironic and sad that although he often jogged in the neighborhood, no one could identify him for eight hours. Not until family members arrived at the medical examiner's office was he identified. He had kept his 5-foot-eleven-inch, 170-pound body in shape by jogging at least thirty minutes every day.

A later report stated, "If Mr. M had checked with a heart specialist before going through the rigors of jogging daily, he might have been alive today instead of dead from a heart attack at such an early age, leaving a wife and two children." According to the deputy medical examiner who performed the autopsy, his heart condition probably would have shown up with a routine ECG, but it surely wouldn't have been missed by a specialist in a cardiac stress test. But M, outwardly fit, had not sought medical advice before undertaking his jogging program.

The examiner concluded, "Anyone past age 40 should certainly be cleared before starting a jogging program. And anyone in the 30s who is unaccustomed to exercise (or accustomed) ought to be cleared first."

Many doctors are now recommending that joggers pin their names and other vital information on their sweat suits in case they meet tragedy while loping along city paths and country highways. In a letter to the *New England Journal of Medicine*, doctors reported that treatment for two joggers was impaired because no one knew who they were. One had been struck by a car, and the other had a burst blood vessel in the brain (ruptured cerebral aneurysm).

Doctors Morris Rossman and Roberto Carvejal of the Delaware Valley Medical Center in Bristol, Pennsylvania, recommended that joggers "wear an identification tag with their name, age, address, telephone number, known medical conditions, medications, and allergies."

4
WHAT IS YOUR FITNESS AIM?

Are you fit? It all depends on whether you can meet the demands of your environment. If you're a fireman, I would call you unfit if your legs aren't sturdy enough to climb a tall ladder. If you're a policeman, you need to be able to get into your squad car and chase a getaway at 80 or 90 miles an hour. Are you a surgeon? I would not consider you fit if your hands trembled while making an incision—even though the rest of your body was functioning normally. Are you a physician? You're unfit if you can't hear or see well.

You will have to stand back and look at yourself and make an honest determination of whether you are meeting the demands of your environment. If not, you will decide on the best method to ensure fitness for your work.

The first step in reviewing your health liabilities and assets is to consider your way of life—your habits, many of which might be threatening to your existence. I'll mention some threatening habits, though not in order of their importance:

- Do you eat too much or too little?
- Are you becoming a chronic alcoholic?
- Is cholesterol fouling your liveliness?
- Do you drive with heavy foot on the accelerator?
- When your body signals trouble, do you procrastinate before taking appropriate measures?
- Do you overwork?

- Are you bored?
- Do you overexercise?
- Do you smoke?
- Do you live in abnormal tension?

If you take an honest inventory, you will find that many of these threats can be neutralized. And even a short consideration of your fitness state will reveal that correcting one or more of these factors is more important for attaining fitness than jogging all over the landscape.

Do you eat too much or too little? It's true that jogging often helps weight loss, but you will admit there are still thousands of joggers, at it for months or years, who bounce up and down, layers of blubber still clinging to them as they exert. Are you in this category? Then ask yourself why you should subject your body to the rigors of jogging. You can't be fit no matter how many miles you run daily.

Are you becoming a chronic alcoholic? Consider Joe—and there are hundreds of thousands like him—who can't wait until he finishes jogging so he can reach into the refrigerator for a beer, or make haste to the bar to mix himself a martini or two. Fitness? Perhaps. But I've seen joggers like Joe who already had the telltale knobby feel of livers becoming cirrhotic. If you jog to be fit yet are an alcoholic, better jog down to Alcoholics Anonymous instead of taking your favorite trail.

Of course, making the diagnosis of alcoholism is difficult. The borderline between social drinker and alcoholic is a thin line. Our Joe is a man who considers himself to be a social drinker. He prides himself on holding his liquor and "never missing a day of work." Yet, he puts away two or three martinis and a bottle of beer at lunch every day. He takes a few slugs from a bottle kept in his drawer so the afternoon will not drag on. He's at the bar of the train he takes home every night. He takes a few highballs before or after dinner. If there's a cocktail party or some celebration, he is the first and last to hang around the bar.

Tell Joe he's drinking too much and he will laugh at you. Besides, he says, "I exercise and keep in trim. I'm as fit as most men my age."

Is cholesterol fouling your lifelines? Perhaps you're not even aware that your cholesterol and triglyceride levels are way above normal. You haven't had a checkup in years. Why see the doctor when jogging keeps you feeling and looking so fit?

Do you drive recklessly? People go about killing themselves in various ways. No matter how fit you are otherwise, the tangled body of a car in a smashup doesn't respect the trimness of your waist any more than the fat one sitting next to you.

Do you procrastinate? The pain in your stomach? The indigestion? The chest pain? The cough? One or all of these symptoms is signaling, is waving red flags that there's some sort of trouble brewing. All your physical fitness will not help you overcome whatever it is that's bothering you unless you find its origin as soon as you can. Disease waits for no man or woman. It will stretch you out, fit or unfit, unless you stomp it out yourself.

Do you overwork? Did work ever kill anybody? You bet it has. And it will kill you even quicker if you come home "dead tired" and decide to get in a few miles of running to wipe out the fatigue. What you do on "second wind" is sufficient to lay you low. Fatigue is a signal to quit rather than to turn on your muscles for more production of lactic acid.

Are you bored? A good hobby is a better antidote than running yourself into the ground.

Do you overexercise? Don't depend entirely on a stress test to tell you how much you can safely exert.

Do you smoke? If you do, you've stumbled on the daddy of all killers. Whatever else you do to get fit, smoking will nullify all your efforts.

Do you live in abnormal tension? You'll have to step out of your skin, take a few steps back, and look at yourself objectively, in your office and in your home. Unless you can find ways to lessen the tight cord of tension that ties you up every day, it's unlikely that fitness is something you can brag about having.

SPECTATION

During an address at a dinner of the National Football Foundation, President John F. Kennedy coined the word "spectation." "The sad fact," he said, "is that it looks more and more as if our great national sport is not playing at all, but watching. We have become more and more, not a nation of athletes, but a nation of spectators. . . . The result of this shift from participation—if I may coin a word—spectation is all too visible in the physical condition of our population." The president believed that the remedy lay in one direction: "in developing programs for broad participation in exercise by all our young men and women."

It is true that the child develops his muscles in natural play as he grows up. But that is not enough. The grade schools and high schools should put more emphasis on the need for physical development. I believe that a token course in calisthenics once or twice a week is not the answer. And how about our colleges? In many institutions, only the freshman is required to participate in physical development. As an upperclassman, he is on his own, which means getting physically lazy prematurely.

I am all for youth fitness and physical development in our youngsters, but I draw the line for middle-aged athletes. I am not carried along with the near-hysteria which has been developing that "if you don't exercise you'll get a heart attack."

I'd like more definite proof that the normal-weighted man or woman who is content to get exercise by a walk around the block is in more danger than his overweight neighbor who prides himself on doing pushups or jogging daily. We don't know enough about the solution of the cholesterol and atherosclerosis problems to be so dogmatic in blaming lack of exercise for so many cardiac ills.

The spectation that President Kennedy so deplored serves a purpose. The halfback who streaks down the field for a touchdown is not the only one who benefits physically and emotionally. Fifty thousand more-or-less spectators who jump to their feet, scream, screech, and pound each other on the back are not only exercising their vocal cords; their pounding hearts and bellows-like lungs belie that. And it's not just that this apparently "inactive" physical participation benefits them. Think of the emotional release. Spectation is not as bad as it appears to be.

THREE BODY TYPES

Some of us need more exercise than others; it depends upon your body build. Each one of us falls into one of three body types, or mixtures thereof. Stand before a full-length mirror and determine into which classification you fit as a body type:

1. Are you an ectomorph? Lean, hungry, thin, and wiry? Long hands, small thin bones, thin calves and thin chest? If so, it's likely your friends say, "You lucky so and so. You eat all you want without putting on an extra ounce. You don't lift a finger in exercise, yet you always look fit."

2. Are you a mesomorph? Square body, broad shoulders, large bones, muscular neck, arms and legs? You are a natural candidate for exercise. Chances are you'd almost die of boredome if you had to sit still for a few hours.

3. Are you an endomorph? Large, soft body, thick neck, prominent breasts? Arms and legs short, fat and heavy? Trunk long? It's likely you are unusually endowed with the philosophy of physical inactivity. You hate to move. You border on masochism when you subject your unwilling muscles to the strain of physical exertion.

If you are an ectomorph, you need not go out of your way to exert. If you are a mesomorph, be wary of overexertion to find fitness. If you are an endomorph, chances are you need a little more exertion, even if you have to bear the discomfort of an occasional turn around the block.

Whatever your body type, it isn't essential that you become a middle-aged athlete. "When you're pushing 50," Bill Leary, who wrote *Graffiti*, said, "that's exercise enough." I think 40 should be the beginning of awareness that exercise should be taken in measured doses.

I was surprised to learn that Neil Armstrong, the first man on the moon, never jogs, does pushups, or plays handball. He said, "I believe that every human being has a finite number of heartbeats available to him, and I don't intend to waste mine running around doing exercises." Saving people's heartbeats has been an obsession of mine for years. I'm glad that a man on the moon agrees.

These heartbeats are your money in the bank. Every day you live you make withdrawals. Unfortunately, you can't make any additional deposits in your account. Get out your pen and pad, or your calculator, and use simple multiplication: 70 beats a minute every 60 minutes each 24 hours add up to about 100,000 heartbeats a day. Carry on the multiplication: 365 days a year for 70 years require 2,575,440,000 beats. Physical and emotional activities increase the number of heartbeats, however, so throw in an extra half billion or so beats to use for extraordinary withdrawals, such as running to catch a bus, illness, or arguments.

Advocates of jogging have told me that this heartbeat bank of mine is ridiculous. They say you can make additional deposits of heartbeats. Their contention is that jogging will slow the heart's rate and increase it's efficiency by increasing the heart's stroke volume. True. But I'd rather not gamble on dropping dead while on the way to the bank to make such deposits. I'd rather respect the number of beats that have been placed on deposit in my life account when I was born.

I known many who believe that the efforts put into jogging will negate many of their bad habits—smoking, taking too many highballs, eating too much, living in a knot of daily tensions, taking pills for hypertension, or working 12 or 14 hours a day. Whatever benefits that may accrue from jogging are unlikely to make up for such profligacy in throwing away millions of heart beats that would have given you added months or years of life. Therefore, your responsibility is to save your heart beats without being too penurious. Whatever your aims in fitness, remember that whatever you were, whatever you are, whatever you hope to be, all's dependent upon the beat of your heart.

I am not alone in the belief that in the search for fitness, many overlook the basic fundamentals. In October 1975, *American Medical News*, a publication of the American Medical Association, ran an editorial on just this point. It was entitled "Killing Themselves":

> Try to keep your temper as you lecture again to those patients who are killing themselves. Of course he smokes, overeats, drinks too much. You know perfectly well she isn't taking the drugs you prescribed. Why? No one knows.
>
> But there they are, taking up your time and stealing it from other patients you might help. It is an irrational world.
>
> The other day in New York [at a conference of the American Health Foundation] cardiac surgeon Michael E. DeBakey reported that many of his patients who recover from serious disease show a tendency to resume the lifestyle that got them into trouble in the first place. . . .
>
> Other speakers cited a long list of irrationalities in the way humans punish their health while seeming to worry about it. . . .
>
> This doesn't help you much as you hear again that the smoker's cough persists, that the drinker's hand still trembles.
>
> The only suggestion is to keep talking, to remember that once in a while a patient listens to his physician's advice."

Ask any doctor, your own doctor, if it isn't true that a greater part of his day is taken with trying to convince patients to stop killing themselves. At the same time, it is ironic—and often tragic—that so many physicians still prescribe the blanket treatment of exercise, for so many of their patients, many of whom aren't psychologically temperamentally, or physically prepared for such exertions.

If I seem to indict anyone in favor of jogging, I must say I have no personal animosity for its proponents. "Exercise: Good or Bad?" was the title of the Physical Fitness Seminar arranged in April 1969 by Stanford A. Lavine, M.D., of the District of Columbia Medical

Society. I was invited to speak on the negative aspects of exercise.

The other three members of the panel, who spoke in favor of exercise, are distinguished physicians: Richard L. Bohannon, M.D., formerly Surgeon General of the U. S. Air Force, then president of the National Jogging Association; Samuel M. Fox III, M.D., chief of the Heart Disease and Stroke Control Program, U. S. Public Health Service; and Acorse W. Thompson, M.D., consultant to the National YMCA and fellow of the American College of Sports Medicine.

Frankly, when I accepted the invitation to appear on the panel with these gentlemen I wondered if I'd get out of Washington alive! But they were kind to me, as I tried to be to them, and the result was a meeting of the minds, in which it was agreed that exercise in moderation never hurt anyone, but that overexercise can be dangerous for some, just as underexercise can be for others. I think we all agreed that the best thing to exercise is discretion.

SOME PRACTICAL OBSERVATIONS

Before you make any quick judgments and disagree about what you think are my views about jogging I hope you will consider the following practical observations on the problem of exercise:

• Exercise is like a two-edged sword. If you love it, practice it moderately, within the limits and capabilities of your physiological age and your fitness for that particular form of exercise.

• I recommend walking, bowling, golfing, tennis, swimming, cycling, mountain climbing, gardening, sking, and scores of other physical activities—all with sensible moderation.

• However, if you practice exercise "to the limit" with fits and spurts, it can become potentially harmful. To put it bluntly again, yes, sometimes it can kill.

• If you hate exercise, if you were born physically lazy, if exercise isn't fun, forget it. You can become just as fit by learning and practicing the measures I have already mentioned for attaining fitness: by living in less tension at the office and at home; by learning how to relax; by keeping your weight normal; by tending to your blood pressure, blood lipids, and blood sugar; by quitting tobacco; and by drinking moderately, if at all. Your ordinary daily activities will provide the exercise you need for fitness.

• Whether you love exercise or hate it, being fit and in good health depends basically on knowing your physical, emotional, and mental capabilities and limitations. Discovering these things is reason enough for periodic cardiac checkups.

• It is a misconception that athletic fitness and good health are identical. It is entirely untrue that a fit body precludes serious illness. The fact is that the little microbes respect exercisers no more and no less than they do those who sit at a desk all day.

• If you are a middle-aged athlete, do not be conscience stricken about slowing up. I agree with Russell Lynes who wrote, in Look magazine: "Middle-age confers the right to quit before exhaustion. . . . There's nothing unvirile about resting between sets of tennis when you are in your 40s, whereas in your 30s it would be a minor sort of disgrace."

• It has been said that the overworked dog or horse grows prematurely old. So it is with a man or woman. In his studies of humans as well as of flies at Johns Hopkins about thirty-five years ago, Dr. Raymond Pearl found evidence that those who avoid too strenuous exercise after 40, and do not engage in heavy muscular activities, have a much better chance of long life than the misguided middle-agers who overtax themselves. Over twenty-five years of observing patients has convinced me of this truth. I believe that too many of us commit slow suicide by overexertion. (Joggers tell me Dr. Pearl's is an old theory. So is the law of gravity!)

• There is no undisputed proof that exercise is a prevent-all or a cure-all. It underwrites no guarantee against heart attacks or for longevity. Be alert that you may be exercising a heart that has suffered a silent coronary attack. Although I agree that movement and exertion are vital as we go about our daily chores, keep remembering that too much exertion can be as fatal as too little.

• An editorial said in the December 12, 1977, issue of the *Journal of the American Medical Association* in part, "There are an estimated

300,000 deaths in the United States each year as a result of coronary disease. Most of these deaths occur outside a medical facility before the subject obtains medical care. Ventricular fibrillation, which is believed to be responsible for the majority of such sudden deaths, may occur during strenuous physical activity."

Before you turn to our guide to help you discover whether you are, by nature, physically lazy or physically active, I hope you will take a few minutes to reread the previous list of practical observations on the problems of exercise.

If you balance my suggestions against the prevailing theories of the pro-exercise enthusiasts, I think you will agree there is room in our society for a moderating force to neutralize the burgeoning excesses of overactivity. Perhaps you will ask yourself, for the first time, "I wonder if it's possible that I may be jogging unnecessarily?"

DO YOU JOG FOR FITNESS?

Do you jog? Perhaps you don't know the reason. But reason there must be. You will discover it if you look for it. Often the answers are evident if you ask yourself the following questions:

Have you been born physically lazy or active?

Is exertion a need for you? Do you find physical inactivity a bore?

Are you ashamed of being caught in a rocker?

Do you disdain taking a daily nap?

Have your friends or your doctor influenced you to jog?

Are you concerned that inactivity will weaken your heart?

Have you been convinced that exercise and longevity are inseparable?

Do you believe that jogging will keep you young?

Evident answers aren't invariably correct ones. You may have to dig deeper for reasons stored away in your subconscious. The mind and brain are jealous of revealing their secrets.

I believe I can help unlock your reasons for jogging. I've picked them up by talking to joggers of all kinds: executives, carpenters, physicians, lawyers, shop workers, secretaries, editors, sales people, cooks, students, and homemakers. If you read the following short case histories, you may find among them a mirror image of yourself, and your own reasons for jogging will rise to the surface, easily recognizable:

The robot. She is a pretty 25-year-old office worker whose job is to punch a computer. Her work is mechanical and tiring. Her life is mechanical, she says. So is her jogging.

"Why do you jog?"

"No special reason," she said. "Everybody's doing it. I consider myself some kind of robot, like the machine I work on in the office. So when I get home, I punch an internal switch which automatically makes me take off my clothes and jump into trunks and sneakers. Then I jog until I get tired. And go to sleep."

The fat one. "Look at me and you'll have the answer," said this 42-year-old homemaker. "I weigh 182, at least 45 pounds over-weight. I've tried to lose. I've read every diet book ever written. But nothing has helped. I've been jogging for about a week, hoping it will help shed the pounds."

Have you lost any weight?"

"Not any to speak of, yet. But I'm hoping!"

The depressive. A middle-aged businessman, he had been advised by a friend to jog because he had been depressed lately. Had he been to a psychiatrist? No, but he had read recently that some psychiatrists had been advising jogging for some of their depressed patients.

After months of jogging, he became more depressed. A psychiatrist later discovered that he suffered from manic-depressive psychosis. Lithium relieved him more than his previous exertions on the jogging path.

The nervous one. "I'm not surprised that you've asked," said a 35-year-old editor of a national magazine. "I'm sick and tired of taking tranquilizers for my nerves. They make me feel like a zombie. I understand that jogging is the best kind of balm for jittery nerves. I've been at it just a few days. Let's see."

The middle-aged athlete. "I had my fortieth birthday last week. I asked myself, why I should let myself deteriorate? I'm not yet ready for the old folk's home. I was a four-letter athlete in school. Why shouldn't I keep myself in shape? That's why I jog."

I asked, "How about taking long walks?"

He said, "Not competitive enough. When I jog I compete with myself to keep running even after I'm exhausted."

The insomniac. "I used to be up most of the night because of my night sweats," she said. "My doctor refuses to prescribe estrogens. He doesn't want me to get cancer of the uterus. So he suggested that I jog."

"How has it worked out?"

"Some nights I sleep, but others I'm awake because jogging tires me out too much."

The tired one. "I'm always tired lately. I know the reason. Instead of jogging only a mile or two a day, I've been swallowing the whole bottle instead of taking it in teaspoonful doses. I run at least five miles every day. I'm celebrating my sixtieth birthday. I'm beginning to believe there's no fool like an old fool."

The headache. "My migraine has been killing me. As a school-teacher, I'm under greater strain than most people realize. Eight-year-olds finally get to you. A friend says that jogging is good for headaches. Don't you agree?"

I said that I've known some patients under great nervous pressure who have released some of their tension by walking, jogging, or taking some mild form of exercise. But what's important is to find out what kind of headaches are the more common "tension headaches," exercise may relieve some of the unrelenting tension suffered by some patients.

The lonely one. The timid young secretary confessed, "I know my weakness. I'm afraid to be alone. I live by myself and have difficulty meeting people. I've seen pictures of joggers passing each other and waving, and crowds of runners, shoulder to shoulder at the beginning of marathon races. I think these pictures, more than anything else, influenced me to take up jogging."

"How has it worked out?", I asked.

"I'm having dinner with a girl I met on the jogging course. That's a start at least."

The masochist. "I don't know of anything that gives me so much innocent pleasure than jogging," said this burly, serious-faced machine-worker. "I admit what I like is the pain of it. I jog so hard and so long until I get pain in my chest, cramps in my belly and legs, and wonder what I'm doing there. Then I know. It's because I actually enjoy pain. I admit I'm a masochist."

Lack of appetite. "I started to jog to increase my appetite. I quit because I kept losing weight. My appetite after running is practically nil. I was surprised. I always believed that exercise increased appetite."

The poetic one. "I jog to be one with nature," said the college freshman. "Believe it or not, when I can commune quietly with nature, I can compose poems in my head. I can't wait to jog home so I can put them down on paper." She paused and said, "Don't you think every writer should jog?"

The people-hater. "At work I'm surrounded by humanity. As one friend said, in summer it's not the heat and humidity that get you down—it's the heat and humanity! Most of the time I want to get away from people. I find the best way to do so, without insulting them, is to jog. You're all alone with your own thoughts and don't have to listen to silly nonsense." He looked at me meaningfully, bent down to tie his laces, and loped off—alone at last.

The failure. "There's something about jogging that boosts your spirit. I've often felt, what's the use of going on? I'm nothing but a failure. But after jogging a while, I begin to feel better. The very fact that I'm alive and well enough to throw my legs about proves that I'm not a complete failure as a human being."

The successful failure. "I have all the money I need, own my business, and have a fine family. Yet, deep down I'm dissatisfied. I've taken up jogging to clear my mind. So far it hasn't worked. I guess I need a psychiatrist."

The doctor-jogger. My 38-year-old colleague had just finished his nightly turn around the quarter-mile track on the university campus. "That makes three miles. I usually jog at least five miles three times a week, but a knee sprain has slowed me up this week."

He looked as smug and self-satisfied as if he had just completed a long stint in the operating room. Then he looked down his nose, smirked, and said, "How in hell can you stay so lazy? Why don't you get off your rear end and run for a change?"

I said, "Still trying to convert me? When will you be satisfied to let us lazy guys live out our contemptible lives in peace? At least, as a doctor, I can stand up to you and say 'Not for me.' But how about your lazy patients? Think how many you've condemned to an exertion they hate, simply because you've convinced them that exercise is good for them. And not simply good, but actually essential to save their heart from slowly disintegrating from disuse."

He looked at me quizzically. Then as if to challenge me, he said, "I think I'll do another mile. No charge for admission." He started off wearily, not only to convince himself, but me, that he was no ordinary man. Macho! Macho!

The youth searcher. A sad sight, both front and rear: face overpainted and overpowdered, and buttocks overfilling her running trunks. At last, driven off the road by a dog barking at her heels, she stopped next to me. She was at least 65.

"Why do you jog?" I asked.

"What better way to stay young?" she said.

The strong-heart seeker. One of the common reasons why so many jog is the belief that it will save their heart. When joggers say that is the reason for jogging, I tell them that there is no specific scientific evidence that jogging saves hearts.

"But my doctor says so."

"Do what he says," I offer. "But tell him you've met at least one doctor who disagrees."

The hypertensive. It's natural for patients to seek shortcuts to health. Many who jog do so because they've heard that jogging will lower high blood pressure. Undoubtedly, this occurs in many people. But what I tell them is that this is only a temporary result. For specific and continuing control of hypertension, I advise that they rely on drugs and other therapy than jogging.

The heart attack victim. "I had a coronary attack two months ago. My doctor advises that I jog to strengthen my heart. Frankly, it scares me." He looked at me as if expecting a negative reply, that would reinforce his fears about jogging after a heart attack.

All I could say was, "It scares me, too. But listen to your doctor. I don't want to disrupt your relationship as patient and doctor working together to keep you well."

Extroverts and introverts. The former run because they like to meet new people; the latter because it gives them the opportunity to get away from people.

Endmorphs, ectomorphs, mesomorphs. Each of these old friends has something different to say about the malady. Endomorph: "I hate it. Why I jog I don't know." Ectomorph: "I can take it or leave it. I keep fit without it." Mesomorph: "I love it. I love it. I love it. There's nothing like a workout you get from jogging. I feel alive."

The undeveloped one. "I have skinny legs. I hope it will round them out."

The family jogger. Both husband and wife, surrounded by four young child-joggers, said, "There's nothing like jogging to keep a family together. We jog every Sunday."

"What happened to all the bikes you used to ride together every Sunday?" I asked.

They shrugged their shoulders as if to say bike-riding was getting to be passe. "Jogging is the thing."

The golf klutz. "To tell you the truth, doctor, I've given up golf because I'm a klutz. I've played over twenty years and haven't yet broken a hundred. When I jog, I feel that I'm as capable as the next fellow."

The pulse-taker. "I've always been a pulse-taker, even when sitting and relaxing. Now that I have to check my pulse while jogging, I don't feel so silly always taking my pulse."

The so-I'll-drop-dead! "If I go, that's the way I'd like it. Fast, and while I'm jogging."

The sweat and stink of it. "If you'll pardon the expression, I jog because I like the sweat and stink of it."

The joiner. "I can't say no when asked to join any kind of organization or lodge. When a friend suggested that I join a jogging club, what was I to do? Frankly, I hate exercise. But I couldn't let him down."

The personality seeker. "I've read that jogging will help improve a person's outlook on life and personality. That's why I took it up. So far I haven't noticed much change, but I'm persevering."

YOUR FITNESS AIM

In a life in which few can escape emotional and physical discomforts, why include activities you hate? For everyone who enjoys jogging there are thousands who hate it. In aiming for the bull's-eye of fitness, you should never feel that you are forcing yourself to exercise. You may be in better physical shape than you realize. You needn't climb mountains or run a marathon to prove to yourself that you are fit.

For those born lazy, exercise is an obnoxious and dirty word. If you're honest about it, you'll admit that bending over to pick the newspaper from the front lawn is a tiring effort. I have a friend who sold his sports car simply because getting in and out of the car was an uncomfortable exertion.

My friend is not alone in being allergic to exercise. At least 100 million Americans are physically lazy and refuse to participate in any fitness program.

Depend on a vigorous rubdown after a shower; putting on and taking off your clothes; carrying bags of family groceries; a daily walk—and scores of other daily activities, which are often over-looked, to keep you as fit as you need to be to enjoy life.

5

HOW THE HEART REACTS TO ANXIETY AND EXTREMES OF EXERTION

He was struck down by a heart attack at the age of 38 while jogging. Fortunately, medical help was near, and he recovered after his heart was defibrillated. He recovered satisfactorily and returned to active law practice and weekend golf. Although his doctor said he could return to jogging, he refused.

He was still apprehensive about having intercourse. Once or twice weekly used to be his average indulgence. Now that fear has taken over, he wonders if he is inviting another attack by having intercourse as seldom as once a month.

There are many like this young attorney. If you have simliar problems in your family, remember that each patient is a problem unto himself. You can understand why this is true. Only your own doctor can truly make an estimate of what is harmful. It will depend on what your checkup reveals and on how you react emotionally and physically to sexual activity. However, you should know that the well-compensated, strengthened heart should be no deterrent to the sex act. Your heart can withstand quite a bit of exertion.

I have been referring to intramarital sexual activity. The usual excitement is somewhat tempered by the sympathetic understanding and collaboration of a wife who is concerned about her husband's continuing health. By unspoken understanding, extremes of exertion are curtailed without lessening enjoyment.

However, I must warn you of an unsuspected threat to life itself when the man with a weak heart engages in extramarital sexual activity. It is potentially dangerous. Many an apparently harmless liaison has ended tragically in some motel or hotel room. Reports indicate that two out of three such heart attacks occurred during or after extramarital exertions and excitement.

Why should this be so? Likely, it is a result of the increased emotional stress induced by guilt and anxiety. Add undue emotional and physical stress to an already weakened heart, and this is an implicit invitation to a heart attack.

When will it occur? Where? Nobody knows, but there is always the threat that extramarital sex is exceedingly dangerous for the heart patient. I'm not being moralistic. Just telling it as it is.

JOGGER APPREHENSIVE ABOUT SEX

It is natural for people who have suffered a heart attack to be apprehensive about having sex. A 47-year-old insurance executive said, "I suppose one can consider that sexual activity is a form of stepped-up exercise. So the question naturally arises, Is it all right for me to engage in sex? I had a heart attack two years ago. I recovered well enough to be able to jog about a mile a day. I have no angina or evidence of a weak heart. My doctor says it's all right." I told him I voted yes with his doctor. Anyone well enough to jog can safely have sex. So can anyone who can negotiate a flight or two of stairs without getting short of breath or having chest pain.

Real apprehension about having sex should arise, as I've said, when extramarital sex causes guilt and tension to overload the coronary arteries or precipitate ventricular fibrillation in a fatigued and extremely irritable heart muscle.

The best way to treat the sexual problems in the heart patient is to keep the lines of communication open between patient and doctor. If your doctor does not initiate the discussion about sex, don't hesitate to tell him you're as much interested in that as in his directions about drugs, diet, and exercise. He will tell you that most heart attack patients are able to have sexual intercourse in about two or three months.

There's no reason why you should be kept uninformed, why you should remain frustrated, fearful, and baffled. One engineer in his late thirties, came complaining that his wife refused sexual relations because she was fearful he might have a fatal heart attack. He began to masturbate. This was more injurious to his heart than normal sex. He became so nervous that he needed tranquilizers. Only after a careful explanation to his wife was intercourse tried again.

Anxiety is a normal post-heart-attack complication in both husband and wife, but it must be recognized and brought into the open. In many patients such a discussion can prevent the onset of secondary impotence following the heart attack. According to some estimates, impotence runs between 10 and 30 percent following coronary attacks. Many cases might have been prevented had the doctor begun early to defuse the fear that normally arises after myocardial infarction.

Anginal pains during sexual intercourse naturally frighten the patient. The thought of having such pains and a possible heart attack often causes impotence or at least prompts the heart patient to limit sex to once a month or less, even though the previous appetite might have supported biweekly or triweekly intercourse. If you will discuss this with your doctor, he will tell you how to use nitroglycerine. When taken immediately before sex, nitroglycerine is usually efficient in preventing chest pains and removing the overlying anxiety. It allows both patient and partner to return more quickly to a level of sexual enjoyment approximating that experienced before the heart attack.

A hard-pumping heart may frighten the patient. Another drug often prescribed by doctors, propranolol, may produce less forceful heart contractions. Skips may also cause anxiety. Antiarrythmic drugs will help this discomfort.

Perhaps most important of all are the understanding, patience, and consideration of the patient's marriage partner. Often the woman who has had a heart attack fears penetration, and the sick husband fears impotence. Gentleness and faith during the critical period of convalescence lay strong groundwork for the renewal of previous sexual satisfaction.

You will note that I said "the woman who has a heart attack." Although not common before 40 in women, coronary attacks increase after menopause.

WHY PATIENTS DIE IN BED

Often I am asked by disbelieving overexerters, "Isn't it true, doctor, that more people die of heart attacks while sitting or while lying in bed? How do you account for that?"

I answer this way: I have always asked patients who suffered heart attacks—or their survivors—about their physical activities twenty-four or forty-eight hours preceding the attack. In most instances, even though the attack came on during rest, the victims overexerted the day or two previously.

One man carried three heavy suitcases up a long ramp following a train journey. Another shoveled snow. Another jogged. Still another played "too much tennis with youngsters." The most serious case of coronary thrombosis I ever saw occured while the patient was in bed. He admitted to carrying four or five heavy trash barrels out to the curb the night before, even though he knew he had angina pectoris. In hundreds of instances over the years, I learned there was a definite history of unusual exertion within hours of the heart attack.

Always remember that jogging or any other exertion may be risky simply because the exerciser may have had a "silent heart attack" some time ago and hasn't had a complete heart evaluation since. Overexertion can sometimes produce fatal results.

Adding to the findings by researchers at Mount Zion Hospital and Medical Center in San Francisco (mentioned earlier in the chapter "Jogging? For Horses!"), a study of the circumstances surrounding instantaneous deaths of twenty-seven heart victims, four died while running or jogging, another died on the handball court; two were doing calisthenics, another was digging a ditch, and still another was carrying a heavy object. The researchers observed that although some physical activity enthusiasts take reassurance from the fact that they've been jogging or playing handball for years, but many of the victims died seconds after performing activities they did frequently. For example, one man had jogged a mile every morning for five years. He dropped dead returning one morning from a customary run.

Call me a spoil sport for telling you all these gruesome details. I realize that taking exercise from the middle-aged athlete—especially if he is a jogger—is like taking candy from a baby. But as the parent says to the child, "It's for your own good." How could I be aware of the dangers without warning you?

HOW TO HARNESS YOUR HEART POWER

Whether you are hearty or heartsick, your heart power is God's most precious gift. Cherish it. For it is true that you can't have peace of mind or peace of soul without peace of heart. Upon the efficiency of your heart depend the well-being and effectiveness of every one of the many billion cells that make up your body. When you breathe, your heart is the source of oxygen exchange. When your brain spins webs of thought, you can thank the efficiency of that amazing pump called the heart. And so with the liver, kidneys, stomach, and all the rest. As goes the heart, so do they.

Full cooperation with your physician is a necessity if you want to give your heart every chance to continue working for you. I suggest the following precautions as additions to your philosophy of living. If you follow these suggestions, you will lighten the load on your coronary arteries and heart:

• Never overeat. Rest at least one-half hour after eating.

• Try taking a nitroglycerine pill under your tongue BEFORE an exertion similar to one that brought on chest pain previously.

• Never shovel snow. Never run after anything.

- Don't smoke. Stay away from smoke-filled rooms.
- Try to control your emotions. A fit of temper is worse than suddenly overexerting. It has killed many an anginal patient.
- Don't disbelieve the diagnosis of angina your doctor has made simply because the resting ECG was normal. There are other tests. Ask for consultation with a cardiologist.
- If your present job is too much for you—either physically or emotionally—better change it. If you determine to stick it out, you may get stuck.
- Take frequent rest periods and don't try to work off tensions by exerting. Learn how to take naps at the drop of a hat.
- Don't fill up on "fat" snacks before bedtime.
- Moderate walking is good exercise for the heart. Try to increase the distance gradually—and within your limits of pain. This and other graduated exercises, although not severe, will help build new, collateral circulation in the heart.
- You may have a daily ration of two ounces of scotch, rye, bourbon, or brandy and moderate amounts of wine or beer. Moderate drinking may help cut down nitroglycerine needs. But never drink before driving.
- See your doctor periodically even if you feel well. Do as the doctor says, not as he does. Don't wonder why he smokes as he delivers the ultimatum no smoking.
- Don't strain when constipated. If there is no choice, be sure that you keep your mouth open. This lessens strain on the heart.
- If you have a so-called virus, stay home until you are well. If you jump the gun and return to work early, you may weaken your heart. If confined to bed, don't lie immobile too long. Every few hours flex the muscles of your arms, feet, and legs. This will help prevent blood stagnation and complications in the leg veins and lungs.
- When warned against high cholesterol, don't fill up on ice cream, fatty meats, fried food, eggs, cream, pastry, or other saturated fats.
- Don't stay obese. You invite diabetes, high blood pressure, coronary disease, kidney trouble, or stroke.
- Don't be overly ambitious.

- Don't put off a needed vacation.
- Don't nurse chronic resentment.
- Remember that middle-aged arteries become inelastic and arteriosclerotic.
- Check early and often on your blood pressure.
- Don't procrastinate. Don't diagnose or treat yourself.
- Don't eat a stale cheese sandwich and a warm glass of milk off your desktop. Such food may suit a mouse, but not you.
- And last but not least, have faith. When you have heart disease, don't live in daily fear.

BED PRISONERS

Although I believe in lightening the load on the heart wherever possible, I assure you that I'm aware of the dangers of the other extreme—the dangers of overresting the heart. It was not so long ago that most doctors used to point a stiff forefinger at the patient's bed and pronounce the sentence like a judge: Better get into bed and stay there if you know what's good for you. I recall the numbers of "bed prisoners" who used to beg to be let out, but physicians were adamant. Doctors just knew that bed was good for you, and it was our job to enforce the treatment.

That thinking has changed. We have become aware of the dangers of unnaturally prolonged bed rest. As in any science or art, new conceptions take the place of the old. It is better to admit past mistakes in judgment than to hold on to old theories because we hesitate to admit that they have become outmoded.

Most doctors now look upon bed rest as a potential enemy as well as a friend. Years ago we kept many heart patients in bed for weeks and months. Many never got well. They came down with complicating pneumonia, inflammation of the leg veins, embolism of the lungs, enormous amounts of fluid in the chest, and large bed sores. Lying flat and motionless in bed contributed to these complications. These patients also lost calcium from their bones; they developed kidney stones and became weak and listless. They lost appetite and complained of constipation. They grew irritable and fussy and their will to live weakened when they developed serious depression.

Consider how things have changed. The patient operated on for acute appendicitis or gall bladder disease is now out of bed within the first few days, and he is encouraged to walk. He does not have to endure the discomforts of the bed pan; he uses a commode. He sits in a chair at intervals during the day and soon feels himself one of the living community rather than a forgotten, dying hulk.

People associate the bed with severe illness and approaching dissolution. Therefore, when we let a heart attack patient sit in the chair within a few days or weeks after his attack, we not only have a stronger patient physically; but one who is psychologically more resistant to the effects of his disease.

When an elderly patient has a stroke, we do not allow him to lie there like a vegetable until he gets pneumonia or bed sores; we start rehabilitation right away. An important part of such a procedure is getting him out of bed as soon as possible.

Of course, there are times when bed rest is important, but doctors know that the initial rest period must not be prolonged without good reason, It must not be allowed to become weeks of unnecessary bed imprisonment.

The stern forefinger of the doctor still points to the bed, but it is not as stern and unyielding as it was a few years ago when we instructed the nurse or family members to immediately report any patient who was playing hookey from bed rest. I caught many a patient shaving who had strict orders to remain in bed. Often I came upon them sitting fully dressed in their living rooms despite orders to remain in bed.

As I look back, many of these people knew what was better for them than I did. In this world of change, the treatment of disease has been changing, too. Bed rest is no longer the universal prescription for the sick. Keep remembering, however, that overexertion can be as threatening as too much rest.

6
YOU DON'T HAVE TO KILL YOURSELF

Once when Eric Segal was interviewed on television, he seemed less proud of the phenomenal success of his best-seller *Love Story* than of his experience as a runner in the Boston Marathon. Long distance runners share a mystique and pride in their ability to put one leg down in front of the other for agonizing miles on end. The exhilaration and euphoria produced by long distance running or jogging breeds a race of the physically elite. They think they are a race apart. "We distance runners," Dr. George Sheehan observed, "are usually ectomorphs who react to stress with withdrawal. We are ambivalent, moody, and unpredictable. Running provides solitude, contemplation, and a physical activity we do well."

Most of us, however, don't like to make that extra physical effort. One friend tells me that bending over to pick up his daily newspaper from the lawn seems like a needless waste of energy. "It's an effort. I'm just naturally lazy," he says. But it's physical laziness. In his office ten hours a day, he gives his brain a real workout, and he loves it.

It takes more than a relatively high level of physical industriousness to make a dedicated, persistent jogger, however. Without a degree of masochism, or at least a high threshold of pain, few would tolerate the multitude of pains that commonly afflict joggers. Fewer still would subject themselves to the life-threatening rigors of jogging were it not for the distorted view of joggings benefits, exhilarations, and joys that routinely fill the jogging books and periodicals.

Many consider adopting jogging as a way of life because they hear only the descriptions of the beatific, spiritual experiences that many joggers emphasize—at the expense, of course, of more accurate accounts of hours of discomfort and pain. For example, listen to a happy jogger:

> In a society driven by competition, jogging is a refuge. It is a silent pursuit, broken only by the steady rhythm of your breathing and pumping of your heart.
>
> You can do it alone or with a friend. You don't need equipment. You can do it anywhere at any time. Best of all, it gives magnificent physical and psychological benefits. Almost everyone I know has lost weight (or redistributed it), firmed thighs, calves, and buttocks, and increased lung capacity after a few months of daily jogging.
>
> As for the fun involved, why must exercise appeal on a child's level? Part of the benefit comes from the required discipline which gives you a genuine sense of accomplishment. Unlike calisthenics alone, jogging gives you a beautiful sense of movement. In fact, it improves your grace, balance, timing and posture, as well as your self-confidence.
>
> When you run you forget your troubles and clear your mind. It's an ideal time to be alone with your thoughts, too. It makes one appreciative of being alive, well, and healthy. It helped me stop smoking. It helped me eat better, sleep better and relax better. I run about two miles daily.

Hearing such beguiling stories, is it any wonder so many decide to surrender to the blandishments of jogging? But too few frankly discuss the pains and discomforts—aside from the everpresent threat of sudden extinction.

Before I discuss the pain of jogging, I'll make some observations on other promises made for jogging:

A stronger heart? Perhaps. But bear in mind the everpresent danger that the apparently strong heart encounters during jogging. There are, moreover, as I will show you later, less demanding ways of keeping your heart strong.

Prolong youthfulness? Jogging is held out as a means to fool the calendar, but it's unlikely that this is possible.

Fewer backaches? The jarring effect of jogging increases and aggravates back problems. A 52-year-old friend is now on his way to an orthopedist for treatment of displaced disc he sustained during a fifteen-mile run.

Lower hypertension? Temporarily, perhaps, but such exertion should not be substituted for conservative medical management of high blood pressure with drugs and other therapies.

For treatment of high cholesterol and triglycerides? A diet low in saturated fats, combined with moderate exercise, control of obesity, and restriction of high alcohol intake, makes more sense in treatment than depending on a temporary lowering of blood fats by extreme limits of exercise.

Leg muscles stronger? True.

Fewer colds, allergies, and headaches? Untrue.

Face younger looking? If you will carefully study the faces of joggers, you will discover they may be heavily lined, strained, and older looking. Whether you enjoy jogging or not, you can't escape the effects of the strain on your entire body.

Bones less brittle? Likely.

Less appetite? True.

Less constipation? Not true.

Less insomnia? Not invariably. Many are too tired to sleep.

Less interest in sex? This seems to be the majority opinion.

Now let's turn to some reasons why joggers must either be masochistic or have high thresholds of pain.

JOGGING'S PERILS

Stress fractures. Young or old, you may end up in a cast.

Back pain. Hip pain. This is a common aftermath of jogging because of the shock of running, especially on hard surfaces.

Belly cramps. These are common and result from pockets of air in the gut.

Knee and ankle injuries. These joints are often damaged by the strain of running.

Shinsplints. Many runners suffer from shinsplints, in which the pain extends down the front of the legs, below the knee.

Hamstring problems. Tears and pulls in the hamstring muscles are common.

Achilles tendons. Inflammation of these tendons are common in runners and causes severe pain.

Problems of the feet. Heel spurs, blisters, bone bruises, inflamed bones on the soles of feet, and actual factures due to stress are common maladies among runners.

Hypochondria. Runners seem exceptionally prone to hypochondria, perhaps from having the mind turned in so much on the self during running. The meaning of twinges tends to become exaggerated.

A neighbor who jogs tells me that the author of one of the many books on running depicts running as a cure for what ails you, as a key to health, vigor, sound body and mind, happiness, and long life. "Maybe," my neighbor observes, "but personally, I hate to run. Always have. There's the pain. Running gives me pains in my pains. Sometimes the only cure for one day's pain is to replace it the next day with a pain someplace else. Monday morning, I awoke with Sunday's pains in the muscle tissue around my left knee, the left side, and the left groin. For twenty minutes, my feet went chunk, chunk, chunk. When I came back from the run, those pains were gone, but my right big toe, a few hours later, was killing me."

Have you ever heard of "jogger's kidney"? This phrase was coined to describe pseudonephritis or the abnormal presence of albumin, red blood cells, in the urine, which is so common among joggers. According to Dr. Robert Johnson of Knox College, in Galesville, Illinois, large numbers of the country's estimated 8 million joggers have pseudonephritis. Usually, jogger's kidney cures itself within forty-eight hours of ceasing the sport, but it remains undetermined whether this condition can lead to serious kidney damage. Meanwhile, according to a piece in *News from the World of Medicine*, "sports physicians advise fitness freaks to keep on running or jogging." The known benefits, they say, far outweigh any known disadvantages. If I were a jogger and had jogger's kidney, however, it would require more than a handful of sports physicians to convince me to continue. The article reported that

Dr. Herbert L. Fred, of St. Joseph's Hospital in Houston, and a distance runner himself, first noticed blood in the urine. He and Dr. Ethan A. Natelson, academic chief of medicine at St. Joseph's, questioned twelve other runners who had similar symptoms. During or after running the men passed bloody urine, which cleared to normal after three or four voidings.

Medical examination showed the condition to be harmless; the runners remained in good health and continue to run in spite of bleeding episodes. Dr. Fred said the bleeding may be due to the walls of the bladder hitting together. This syndrome seems more common in men than in women. Dr. Fred emphasizes, after negative examination, the runner need not give up his exercise.

If the abnormal existence of blood in the urine is not enough to cure you of jogging, suppose you learned that doctors discovered that after jogging there was an elevation of enzymes in the blood similar to the type of elevation found in the blood of heart attack victims? Creatine phosphokinase (CPK), SGOT and others all increase significantly. Suppose then physicians said that no risks were involved? Would I continue to jog? My answer is still no.

Suppose I developed jogger's whiplash? One 35-year-old jogger described "as if hit in the back of the neck with an axe," but within thirty-six hours this same man was seen jogging the same course while holding his neck. This too would have been enough of a warning to end my jogging—and that of most people who credit themselves with a degree of common sense.

If I were a jogger and had managed to remain well except for "jogger's nipples," an irritation produced by the rubbing of the shirt against skin, my answer might be yes. This condition, which afflicts men as well as women, can be prevented by covering the nipples with Band-Aids or by coating them with petroleum jelly to reduce friction. Otherwise, nipples will be raw, bleeding, and painful.

Few joggers have ever been threatened by man's best friend. Various methods of defense have been suggested—saying "nice doggie" as he nips at your heels; ignoring him; authoritatively saying no; shrieking or flailing your arms; bluffing the dog by bending over as if to pick up a rock. Few, if any, of these techniques are invariably effective. According to the Public Health Service, the dogs most likely to test your mettle are the German shepherd, chow chow, poodle, Italian bulldog, fox terrier, mixed chow chow, airedale, Pekingese, and mixed German shepherd.

Edwin Pope, the Miami Herald's sport editor, has found the neutralizer, "an oversized hickory axe handle, easily obtainable for under five dollars. Very strong, but very light, this provides excellent psychological support while at the same time exerting an apparently tranqilizing effect on all but the most psychotic of man's best friends. Since I began carrying my axe handle, I have not been approached within a radius of less than six feet."

YOU DON'T HAVE TO KILL YOURSELF

In their book *Total Fitness in 30 Minutes a Week* (New York: Simon & Schuster, 1974), Lawrence B. Morehouse, Ph.D. and Leonard Gross put it well:

> In their resistance to exercise, Americans show a certain amount of intuitive sense. Exercise, as it is generally taught and practiced, is not simply boring; it is punitive, dangerous and ineffective. . . .
> Fitness is determined by what you do twenty-four hours a day, how you live, work, sit, walk, think, eat and sleep. It's purpose is to help you enjoy life, not to punish you or make you feel guilty. . . .
> You don't have to kill yourself.

I have been accused of being too biased in my opinions on the problem of exercise and jogging. It is said that I too often cast my vote in favor of the lazy person, rather than for the physically active. And it is true that, throughout the years, while trying to keep an open mind, I have been standing up in opposition to many of my colleagues who follow each other blindly in the belief that exercise is good for practically everybody. I have continued a verbal and written crusade against the constantly recurring exercise fads that have sprung up like mushrooms, poison mushrooms, threatening the health of millions of Americans.

Have I been biased? C. P. Curtis pointed out years ago that there are only two ways to be unprejudiced and impartial: one is to be completely ignorant; the other to be completely indifferent. I plead guilty to both knowledge and interest.

"Death Following Physical Stress" was the title of an editorial that appeared in the *Journal of the American Medical Association* (October 13, 1978). The editorial was signed by Zenonas Danilevicius, M.D., and it said in part:

> There is considerable risk of sudden death in connection with strenuous physical exercise in subjects with manifest or latent cardiac disease. This risk is more prevalent when the person involved had no previous stepwise training or exercise leading to strenuous physical activity. . . .
>
> A lesson to be learned is that such conditions in cardiac patients should be clearly identified; patients should be instructed about possible dangers and reminded not to get involved in strenuous physical activity to which they were not conditioned by long-term training. . . . Sudden death seems to be preventable in at least a number of cases and the best method of prevention is progressive training and gradual adjustment to physical stress.

You can understand why I do not believe in the performance of unnatural physical exertions by those who are unaware of the condition of their heart—and by those who, after 50 weeks of physical inactivity turn two weeks of overactivity into a mad quest of "catch-up" for physical perfection.

Gradually, but surely, commonsense about physical exertions is filtering down into the lay community—and I hope the medical community, too. For example, here is a letter to the editor of a local paper; it was headed, "Joggers, Use Your Heads Too":

> Suddenly there comes the desire to jog. Can we really say it improves the health? People have put themselves in a state of exhaustion during this period.
>
> People are abstaining from proper diet to assume very slender proportions, taking away their energy to lose weight. But the body must have a certain amount of rest and nourishment. Excessive jogging can have severe complications.
>
> Jogging has become a universal disease. People drop everything to run through the streets at a rapid pace. What are they rushing into? What do they expect to accomplish? People must take precautions against overtaxing their resources. . . . Jogging is fun, but we can't all make it. Don't disregard medical rules and regulations.

Good sense about health isn't the sole property of staid medical journals and I'm getting more and more letters that reinforce this impression:

Dear Dr. Steincrohn:

I'm beginning to come around to your way of thinking that exercise is unnecessary for physical fitness. What's good enough for Neil Armstrong, the first man to set foot on the moon, is good enough for me. In answer to a question, he said that he did not believe in taking unnecessary physical exertion to become fit for his duties as an astronaut. In fact, he said something that sounded familiar: that he believed in "saving his heartbeats."

Has he read your theory? I have it here where you say, "I believe that each of us was born with a given number of heartbeats in our heart bank. Some of us, because of poor heredity or congenital illness, were born poor. Others were born rich. Those of us who are fortunate were given an initial deposit of two to three billion heartbeats for a lifetime of living.

What I want to stress is that persons born poor (with fewer heartbeats in the bank) should not indiscriminately throw away those beats in the unnecessary exertion known as exercise. Instead they should become heartbeat misers.

Lately, too, I have been reading articles by other doctors who now warn against too much jogging, bicycling, and the like as possibly being dangerous. I think, at last, I'm turning into a believer of your theory rather than the disbeliever I used to be. Aren't you happy?

B.

Happy? Yes, Mr. B. Whenever I can make a convert out of an overexerciser, I consider it an accomplishment. Jogging? Often harmful. Bicycling? As I've facetiously said, it's the best exercise if you coast downhill. Why do people disdain walking?

As for Mr. Neil Armstrong, I don't know if he had read my theory of saving heartbeats. It's possible that he hasn't, and has arrived at his sensible philosophy of conserving heartbeats because of his apparent intuitive good sense and intelligence.

Whichever way, I am not presumptious enough to believe that I can honestly tell my grandchildren that I had something to do with getting the first man on the moon. But between you and me, I'm secretly pleased.

The following piece *Hazards of Jogging* written by John Lister, M.D., in the *New England Journal of Medicine* (April 27, 1978) offers a comic perspective on the pains of jogging:

> Having noticed the correspondence in the *Journal* on joggers' ailments, I was interested to read a somewhat facetious article in the *Sunday Times* in which a lawyer related his unfortunate experience of this allegedly beneficial pastime. He was well aware that it is supposed to be the cure for all the ills of the flesh, but he was far from convinced that it was and only decided to take it up in a desperate effort to control his weight.
>
> The first day was a disaster. He shambled off into the dawn and ran straight into an overhanging branch, invisible in the half light. Next time, he chose late afternoon, when there was still enough light to see the trees, but the ladies of the village were exercising their dogs, and he found himself sprinting for home pursued by an assortment of collies, spaniels and red setters. Next day he had aching muscles in places where he did not even know he had them.
>
> Two weeks later he chose a bright Sunday morning without a dog in sight. This time, he fell into the river! It had been a frosty night, the towpath was slippery, and in he went, to the delight of several moorhens and a family of water voles.
>
> He therefore retired to bed with cold feet and injured pride, determined to get back to work—but not to jogging—just as soon as the pneumonia subsided.

Sublime? Ridiculous? It all depends upon your viewpoint.

7

BE THANKFUL YOU WERE BORN LAZY

About 25 years ago I met a Hollywood movie producer, and I think I talked him into saving his own life. We were discussing a baby's need for exercise to keep healthy and fit. The movie producer, a kindly, outgoing man of 55 at the time, had this to say: "I've heard of your ideas. I don't go along with them when it comes to giving up strenuous exercise. I consider myself a grown baby that requires activity. I've taken up exercise in a big way. And I've got a heart murmur, at that. I exercise before breakfast and before I go to bed. I even go home to my gym at lunch hour and go through the rigmarole."

I asked him what he meant by the "rigmarole." "Come on over to my house and I'll show you my gym," he said.

I never saw so much paraphernalia outside of a sporting goods store.

There were bars and bells; weighted pulleys and a vibrating apparatus; stationary bicycles and rowing machines; punching bags and boxing gloves; and a muscular trainer who was always at hand to knead, pummel, and massage my new friend's muscles.

"What does your doctor say about your fitness program?" I asked.

"He tells me I have a heart murmur and ought to take it easy. I guess he goes along with your theory that people can overdo exercise. But not so in my case. Otherwise, why should I feel so good?"

I liked this man. But whether I liked him or not, I couldn't leave him without warning him. I said that one day he would go beyond the point of recall. I showed him a letter I had received that very morning from a woman on Long Island. The woman was writing straight from the heart. Her letter was long, but the movie producer read it three times.

The woman's husband had been a counterpart of our friend the producer. He, too, had a completely equipped gym. He, too, had been advised by his doctor to lighten up on his physical activities. But he was headstrong. An extremely successful businessman of 48, he believed he knew what was better for him than anyone else. In spite of hard work put in during the day, he punished his heart muscle and arteries during long workouts in his gym at night. He was an exercise fanatic.

Late one night the woman found him sitting at his rowing machine, slouched over and groaning. He was dead on arrival at the hospital. She ended her letter: "Why, oh why, wouldn't he listen?"

The movie man, accustomed to quick decisions, said, "I'm closing up my gym. From now on it's golf, and that in moderation."

I asked him how he could cut off his exercising "just like that." "I have a confession to make, he replied. I hated it all along. I kept at it for two reasons. First, everybody was doing it. And second, the murmur worried me and I was challenging it."

I received a telegram from the producer on his 70th birthday: "I'm still around, murmur and all. Thanks to you and your letter."

These days there's no need to invest in fully equipped home gyms. If you are exercise minded, join a club. Dan Williams, who writes on business for the *Miami News,* described the exercise club phenomenon in an article that appeared in that paper on June 2, 1978:

> Forget the three-martini lunch. It's now the three-mile jog and massage lunch. Or, the raquetball and steam room lunch—with maybe a honey, strawberry and raw egg cocktail thrown in. Instead of lunching out, businessmen have decided to sweat it out. . . .
> At least a half dozen physical fitness clubs—athletic and

raquet ball—have opened here in the last six months. . . . Steam rooms, saunas, facial parlours, whirlpool baths: everything necessary to make one's own reflection in the uniquitous mirrors look good.

"We want to take the misery out of exercise," says Dan Wardy, membership director. "Its a place where businessmen can come on their lunch hour or on their way home to keep fit." He explains that "each member of the club is given a stress test, has his pulse taken, and his blood pressure and fat percentage measured before he is permitted to begin any program. The exercise program emphasizes strengthening of the cardio-pulmonary system.

The bicycle business is also booming. If you like to ride, fine. But there's no scientific evidence that pushing the pedals prevents myocardial infarctions.

The other day a woman said, "My husband's lazy. Physically, that is. He works hard at his job as manager of a large office, But what gets me is that he is too lazy to mow the lawn or do a few repairs around the house. He'd rather hire someone to do it."

I advised her to let the poor fellow alone. Physical laziness is inborn in some people. She wouldn't blame her husband for being bald, would she? Or being only five-foot six when she'd prefer a six-footer? I told her some people are so lazy by nature that they actually ache all over when they watch another human being pull and push—and expose themselves to physical stress.

Many say, "I'd rather die if my living depended upon hard, physical work." You can feel sorry for such individuals if you are an active person, but you mustn't blame them. I know of no miracle drug that will transform them into active individuals.

WHAT IS MODERATION?

I have been accused of being antiexercise and on the side of those who prefer the lazy life. But I do not close my eyes or ears to the opinions of sensible adults who believe that exercise is good in moderation. For example, consider this letter:

Dear Dr. Steincrohn:

I agree with your thesis that overexertion is bad. If an individual has a heart attack as a result of exercise, this can be fairly called overexertion. Also, I agree that any individual who engages in strenuous exertion should have annual checkups. But in the matter of motivation, and in definition of moderation, I take exception.

I believe you are mistaken in your belief that, by and large, people exercise because they think it is good for them. It's too much trouble, doctor. Join a club, assemble the necessary gear, make an appointment, drive over, change clothes, play for half an hour or an hour, bathe, dress, get back to work or home—this is a big nuisance. More trouble than a man will take because it is good for him. He has to enjoy it, and enjoy it quite a bit, or he will never keep it up. The exercise must be pleasant, or anyone would quickly talk himself out of it.

You describe a few strings of bowling, an hour of gardening, tennis doubles with three other old cronies as "moderate." Well, it seems to me that this is almost too moderate. I contend that if an individual takes annual physicals, and if an individual does not "lay off" for some months, but regularly plays some game— squash, handball, badminton—a few times a week, he is on safe ground if his pulse and respiration return to normal before he can get off the court and pull on a sweat shirt.

I believe, doctor, that regularity of effort and quick recovery are the important things, not the amount of effort involved in exercise. If nine holes of golf or an hour of gardening leave an individual hanging on the ropes, this is immoderate; it is overexertion.

But if an hour of squash or handball leaves the player perspiring but comfortable, and he has fully recovered by the time he takes a shower, then this seems to me to be moderate exercise. (I agree that this "moderate exercise" would kill the man who hasn't picked up anything heavier than a knife and fork for twenty years.)

I am reminded of the instance some twenty-five years ago when a bootlegger of my acquaintance applied for some life insurance. Asked about drinking, he admitted that he drank moderately, and was insured. A few weeks later the agent looked him up and accused him of misrepresenting facts: he had spent two or three months a year in a sanitarium, recovering from delirium tremens.

The bootlegger quickly admitted that he was hospitalized a couple of months every year for DTs—but in his opinion this was "moderate drinking." He said, "If I had spent six to eight months a year in the hospital, that would be immoderate."

I admit that "moderation" is an elastic term—but it depends upon the honest evaluation of the exerciser. Rationalization of the benefits and satisfaction of exercise often influence us to make poor decisions.

I disagree with the statement that "exercise must be pleasant, or anyone would quickly talk himself out of it." My guess is that for every person who loves to jog there are five thousand who hate it. Pleasant or not, most people exercise for the "good it does them"—for the fitness and good health it promises.

I think you will be interested in a letter received from Mrs. E. H., of Salt Lake City, Utah, who writes about the predicament of her "lazy" son:

Dear Dr. Steincrohn,

My son, who is 25 and admittedly lazy, is perplexed over what amount of exercise is beneficial (or necessary) for a young adult in good general health. He has read a book by a Dr. Cooper entitled *Aerobics,* and has become concerned about a regular exercise program. It bothers me, too, and I have decided to seek your advice.

Not liking to run (which Dr. Cooper's book seemingly prefers as an exercise), my son has selected to follow that book's walking program, which states that one mile a day (as I prefer) is a waste of time. To benefit from walking one must hike for at least 4½ days out of the week.

According to Dr. Cooper, to derive any benefit from a one mile walk, one would have to move like a robot rather than a human. So running is obviously this physician's propensity.

Personally, I reject Dr. Cooper's book and his theory, and I'm sad that my son has taken it seriously. To see him try to keep up around a five-mile hike for much of the week seems to me like a futile and miserable form of activity. Especially, since he is so lazy and admits he hates it.

Even our family doctor said that this Dr. Cooper's idea was, quote, "nuts." You'll be interested in what I read about exercise in the *International Medical Encyclopedia* originally published in England under the title of *Pears Medical Encyclopedia,* and written by two British physicians, Drs. J. A. C. Brown and A. M. Hastin Bennett:

"But it is necessary to preserve a proper perspective concerning exercise, since this is one of those subjects to which some people attach a quite disproportionate significance. The idea that, in general, exercise is not only a duty for the sedentary individual but that it has a remarkable effect on the health of the body is a reversal of the truth. . . , and many paralyzed or otherwise immobilized individuals who are quite unable to walk have been noted for their longevity."

The encyclopedia concludes the topic with, ". . . there is no truth to the idea that exercise exerts a magic tonic effect on the body as a whole. So far as the possible connection, dubious as it is, between lack of exercise and coronary thrombosis is concerned, it is quite sufficient if the individual walks for five or ten minutes on his way to and from work."

Another book by a Dr. Tether says, "Most young people who are active probably walk a mile a day." He did not recommend formal exercises and concluded, "the exercise fad has been overdone; pleasurable or productive activity is a better way to get exercise."

Unfortunately, our son feels compelled to follow Dr. Cooper's theory on fitness, even though he dislikes it. He has read parts of (and respects) your book *How to be Lazy, Healthy and Fit,* which you published about ten years ago, but he says that when he is my age that will be fine! But at his age he must keep up an exercise program.

He worries me so. He is always "dead tired." And he looks so thin from all this excessive (in my opinion) walking. But there may be hope for him. I had him read your book again. He said he would go by your advice, since after reading it carefully he is more impressed by your reasoning than by Dr. Cooper's.

LEARN TO BE LAZY

Do you live in constant stress? You don't mind working hard at the office, staying late, and coming home to jog. You take your briefcase home on weekends to work some more. You constantly find ways to keep busy when "official" work is done. How long do you think you can continue this way? You are inviting a heart attack.

Recently I talked with a woman whose husband fitted this picture. She bought him a hammock to relax in on weekends. He considers it a joke and never lies in it. He believes that taking it easy makes him less a man. Macho. Macho. She wonders if he's geared by nature to keep working all the time.

Many active men (and women) become conscience stricken when they are caught relaxing. Come upon such a person lying in a hammock or sitting in a rocking chair and he will make excuses like, "I've just been here only a few minutes. Been working hard."

Why the need for such excuses? Even machines have periods of overhaul and rest from constant use. There is an art in relaxation. Just as the heart muscles rests between beats, it makes good sense to let the mind and body idle along between periods of stress and exertion. Chekhov put it well when he wrote, "I am of the opinion that inner happiness is impossible without idleness."

Immoderate laziness, however, can be as great a problem as immoderate overexertion. Consider this patient's complaint:

Many people don't admit it, but I do: I am probably the laziest man ever created. I simply have an allergy to work—physical or mental. I was born hopelessly lazy. Have always hated work or any kind of physical exertion. I just like to sit.

Believe it or not, I have had thirty-one jobs during the past seven years. I quit working hours before checkout time. I'll quit working right in the middle of something important. I don't mind leaving people in the lurch. Therefore, you can understand why I've been fired so often.

I am 42, am overweight and always tired. Although I sleep a lot I feel as if I have never had enough rest. I do not smoke or drink, but I admit I do overeat.

I went to a doctor five years ago. He found nothing wrong. All he said was, "It's all in your head. You're just lazy and you'll have to talk yourself out of it."

But there's something in my favor. I have been through three marriages, no family to support, no starving children to worry about.

Fortunately, examination revealed an underactive thyroid gland. After a few months of treatment for his hypothyroidism, he changed into a wide awake, vigorous man with a purpose in life.

Was he "born lazy"? Perhaps. But this case history indicates that when the expenditure of energy is either excessively great or extremely low, it merits study by a physician. Immoderation is bad at either end of the energy spectrum.

Although it may be evident to family and associates, many lazy persons are unaware they are lazy. Do you know whether you belong in this category? It's better for you to know and to accept your way of life than believe you are as active as most people. It will help keep you from getting into physical activities you dislike.

Laziness, once recognized, should be accepted without shame or guilt. It is as natural for some as overactivity is for others. The only real problem with inactivity is with unproductive laziness—being both physically and mentally lazy can lead to disaster. To evaluate your physical status, answer the following questions:

1. Are you an endomorph?
2. Do you hop out of bed?
3. Do you crawl out?
4. Is there a rocking chair in your home?
5. Do you run to catch a bus or wait patiently to catch the next one?
6. Do you take daily naps?
7. Do you have lunch at your desk rather than go out?
8. Do you enjoy watching others exert, such as weight lifters or joggers?
9. Do you cheat when helping others move heavy objects?
10. Are you too tired to play ball with the kids?
11. Do you watch TV rather than go out?
12. Do you allow dishes to pile up, letters to go unanswered, and otherwise procrastinate?
13. Can you sit and read for hours?
14. Do you avoid even the less demanding sports, such as golf and bowling?
15. Do you feel more comfortable sitting than moving?

16. Do you daydream?
17. Do you avoid cleaning the car?
18. Do you avoid socializing because, for example, you find it much trouble getting dressed?
19. Do you avoid bending over when you drop a scrap of paper into a wastebasket?
20. Are you vaguely conscience stricken about the thought you may be lazy?

A preponderance of positive replies indicates that you are naturally lazy. As a jogger you would be like a fish out of water.

If your physical propensities are similar to those enumerated in the following letter you will not need to answer a long list of questions to determine whether you are a natural exerter.

Dear Doctor:

We running freaks are not disturbed by the rantings and ravings of the "lazy" extremists. Let them frown on any physical activity that requires expenditure of some added energy. We love it.

The history of the current jogging and running "fad" of the past decade does indeed include some severe heart attacks and even deaths during strenuous exercise. Two of my friends have died while jogging. But other friends of mine have died in bed, too.

I personally would die of boredom within a year if I didn't run. An exaggeration, of course, but you get my point. I am not saying that I know more than you about these matters. But I don't think statistics have been prepared as yet that would enable you, me, or anybody else to evaluate accurately the risks of strenuous exercise—or of the sedentary life.

Here is a brief history of my own career in strenuous running:

Late 1969, age 51: Started slow jogging, walking, and bicycling to calm jittery nerves; couldn't smoke a pipe anymore with my new teeth, uppers and lowers. Decided not to take up cigarettes as a substitute.

Mid 1970, age 52: ten pounds heavier and "feeling my oats." I became interested in the burgeoning Masters' running movement. Began more strenuous training pointing for competition.

March 1971, age 53: Ran one mile in competition—5 minutes, 39.6 seconds.

May 1971, age 53: Ran second mile in competition—5 minutes, 32.2 seconds.

February 1972: Ran 5 miles in competition—33 minutes, 54 seconds.

1972, 1973, 1974: Continued to train daily and compete about ten times per year. Improvement steady. Training 1500 miles per year, with lots of hill climbing and calisthenics. Typical marks: 1 mile—5 minutes, 28 seconds; 5 miles— 30 minutes, 42 seconds; 10,000 meters—39 minutes, 33 seconds; 20,000 meters—84 minutes, 50 seconds.

1975 to 1978: Father time is steadily improving his lead, but slowly. I still train hard and compete very successfully in my own age group.

February 25, 1978, age 60: Ran my first marathon—3 hours, 28 min. Felt good, pulse back to normal two hours later. Cut lawn and jogged 2 miles next day. Back to full training schedule 3 days later.

Doctor, I enjoy competitive running: the camaraderie, the business contacts, the opportunities for economical travel, and so on. Shouldn't these things be weighed against the possible dangers of strenuous exercise after 50? Maybe I'm wrong. What do you think?

J.P.C.

This may surprise you, but if this man were my patient, I'd tell him to keep on. A doctor isn't a little god whose purpose is to make out a life schedule for each one of his patients. All we can hope to do is present whatever facts we have so you can make the choice.

For example, some doctors discharge patients who continue to smoke after they have been advised not to. I do not believe in this. All a doctor need do is inform the patient that he invites emphysema, heart disease, or cancer by smoking, but the patient has the right to make his choice.

And so it is with running, Mr. C. enjoys it so much, how could I possibly ask him to quit? Assuming his doctor finds him in good conditions, he should carry on and enjoy. From the vantages of the physically lazy, one wonders how it can bring Mr. C so much pleasure, but so does Mr. C wonder about a man his age rocking in a chair. It's a matter of viewpoint.

The viewpoint of Ray Will, a long distance runner, quoted in *The Complete Runner* by editors of *Runners World,* is of interest:

> Sometimes I think the purists of our sport lose sight of what it's all about. To listen to them talk, you'd think that running is the passport to eternal bliss on earth. But one look at any runner's reddened face and unsteady pot-race knees tells a different story. Running is work, and hard work at that—and some of us do it so that we may brag to our friends that we ran 20 miles today. . . .

For others, the inner experience of jogging is more significant. The July 8, 1978 *American Medical News* quoted George Sheehan, M.D.:

> The essence of the running game for me is the feeling I get when running alone occupies me. I am comfortable, calm, relaxed, full of running. I feel like I could go on like this forever. I am suspended, content with the nothing. And the peace that comes with it. That is the essence of the running experience for me. The lack of anxiety, the complete acceptance, the letting go and the faith that all will be well. I have no other goal, no other reward. The running is its own reason for being.

Dr. Sheehan, author of *Running & Being:* Simon-Schuster has emerged as the Pied Piper of running and to whom running is a "wordless religion," runs ten miles a day every Tuesday and Thursday. He says, "If you keep on running long enough you're going to become the person you're supposed to be. Everybody's searching for something. With running you no longer need TM and est, Outward Bound and Librium."

Another enthusiast is author James F. Fixx who, writing in *Newsweek* (December 18, 1978), said, "Yesterday, I ran for an hour through a seaside park near my home in Connecticut. . . . By the time I got home I felt refreshed and beatified. I know of no human activity, except perhaps sex, that can do so much in so brief a time, and do it so wonderfully." I thought of John Barrymore's famous quip: "The thing that takes up the least amount of time and causes the most amount of trouble is sex."

According to Dr. Sheehan, fifteen years ago there were about seven marathons a year; now there are more than two hundred. Last year there were 25,000 people who ran a marathon. Boston had 4,000 entries. Dr. Sheehan has run in fifty marathons, which are races of twenty-six miles. In reviewer of Dr. Sheehan's book observed, "For him, body, mind, and soul become one. . . . While running is Dr. Sheehan's sport, he doesn't advocate it for everyone. Run only if there is a runner inside you, Dr. Sheehan says."

Well, I must admit that there isn't a runner inside me. I have accepted myself as I am; I have found refuge in my rocker rather than as in running or jogging. In spite of what millions of running disciples believe, I consider myself as fit emotionally, physically, and philosophically as any dedicated runner. For me, an hour or two in my rocker every day, has brought me calm, relaxation, and peace. Quietly rocking, like running, also lessens anxiety and brings the faith that all will be well.

To the heavenly promises of Dr. Sheehan and others jogging enthusiasts, I contrast the thoughtful observations of Perry R. Ayres, M.D., F.A.C.P., in *Forum on Medicine*, *Them As Can*, November, 1978, the official bulletin of the American College of Physicians. The piece was subtitled "To Many, Jogging Is Exercise, but to Others It Is Simply Masochism."

Allowing that some of his best friends are joggers. Dr. Ayres said his sympathies were with the other side, that he simply does not understand joggers. He mentioned his reaction to a physician who was asked to hold forth on the benefits of jogging while speaking at a medical convention. What turned Dr. Ayres off was the doctor saying that he took up jogging and marathon running because he was fundamentally antisocial. The lecturer remarked that after a hard day at the office, he could strip down to his underwear, put on his Adidas, and run away from people. He said it helped him keep his sanity.

In describing the finish of the Boston Marathon, Dr. Ayres said,

Runners continued to straggle into the Center to mingle with the dispersing crowd. They limped, they grimaced, they held their sides in pain, they vomited, they kneaded cramping muscles, and some cried. Except for the very few who smiled weakly, none showed any sign of satisfaction, of mission accomplished. They lay on the floors and benches, or hobbled about in the company of consoling suporters. The flush of exercise had subsided, and their skin was pale and clammy. . . . A colleague mused, "What a paradox that we [doctors] who advocate exercise were here to witness this exhibition of masochism."

I wondered how often—if at all—running enthusiasts, doctors included, had described similar experiences arising out of marathon races.

The first marathon was run in 490 B.C. by the messenger Pheidippides who ran the twenty-five miles from the plain of Marathon to Athens carrying the news of the Greek victory over invading Persians. According to Herodotus, as Pheidippides reached the end of his exertions, he blurted, "We won!" and fell dead.

When the modern Olympics were being organized, the present length of twenty-six miles, 385 yards was established. The first Boston Marathon was held on Patriots' Day, April 19, 1897. It has been held on that day every year since to commemorate Paul Revere's ride way back in 1775.

According to records, not one runner has ever died while running in the Marathon. How many, unrecorded, unknown, and unsung have died hours or days later?

Fatality or not, most joggers who continue to run—and suffer— are masochistic. Some of my friends who jog resent this label, but one does not have to be a trained physician to know suffering when he sees it. Consider an article by M. Klinkenberg which appeared in the *Miami News* on September 5, 1978. It reported a Labor Day 10,000-meter race (6.2 miles) in which 720 participated.

Several runners stopped because of heat prostration, and a dozen others became sick to their stomachs—but the overwhelming opinion of contestants was that the race was great fun.

Dennis Kasprzyh, the winner said, "The race was very punishing. It is a mental thing—mind over matter."

A 49 year-old runner said, "It is legal foolishness. Every race I feel like quitting. If it's a good race, you want to quit after a mile or two. I thought about quitting at about three miles. You just have to accept the pain. Your mind is wondering why you're doing it and your body is screaming "Stop, stop," but if you do it's even worse. I've quit before and it's not a pleasant experience. The pain you go through the next day is terrible. You keep on telling yourself you know you could have finished."

Another Miamian who has been running for two years said, "It doesn't matter if you win or not. It was a good race. Running is a definite high. It feels so great. It's beautiful."

The race coordinator summed it up this way: "We have a lot of frustrated athletes that take an interest. Even though people are throwing up, they're having a good time."

Masochism: The abnormal getting of pleasure from being hurt or humiliated.

Exercise is painful for those who are lethargic by nature. Watching others strain, push, and pull, whether piano movers or gymnasts, produces vicarious satisfaction, soon superceded by wonder at how many beings can seem so unconcerned by the extra physical effort involved. Discomfort becomes exquisitely painful and unbearable when the physically lazy person finds that his own muscles, ligaments, and bones are involved in physical contortions and strains. Movement is anathema for the physically lazy—perhaps an unconscious realization that it is much better to be relaxed than overactive.

In her syndicated column, Ellen Goodman described the quandary of a jogger who disliked the self-denial of enforced running activity. The woman had dutifully trudged along, fighting the impulse to stop, hoping to experience the "high" and sense of well-being promised for runners. She had been reading about the pleasure to be derived from the process of jogging. But now here she was on this dirt road, under a perfect sky, on a beautiful 75-degree day—yet she felt miserable.

Ending her column, Ellen Goodman wrote, "In one flashing moment, she knew what so many others before her had so long denied. She hated running."

If you are lazy, but still not completely guilt free because so many of your friends jog and put you in the lower echelons of the pecking system, there's still hope for you: Rent a jogger! If you are tired of jogging, of having your ankles ache, your feet swell, and your lungs feel like stretched balloons, hire someone else to do the running for you.

According to UPI, for a modest yearly fee of $1.95, Harry Buonocore of Queens will send you a handsome, hand-lettered certificate that vows he will run a mile for you every day, "in rain or shine, snow or frost." When Harry's under the weather, his four sons help him out. Your 7½-by-12-inch certificate will certify that the bearer has rented a jogger "to secure the following life-enhancing benefits—a healthful glow, extraordinary stamina, exciting muscle tone, and a power-filled sense of total well-being."

I know several lazy nonjoggers who will be buying these certificates for friends as gifts.

PART 2
THE SOLUTION

8
OBESITY CONTROL: THE PILLAR OF FITNESS AND HEALTH

Patients like to pin you down. One asked, "What do you think is our greatest enemy?" He was a heavy smoker and drinker, and he expected me to say smoking or drinking. He sat there unaware that the enemy he thought was his most benign—obesity—was the greatest threat to his health and life.

I explained to him that he was at least forty pounds overweight. He, like most other people, was unaware that obesity is our number one enemy because it is tied in with other threats to our existence: heart disease, hypertension, diabetes, stroke. When you eliminate obesity, you automatically raise barriers of defense against serious illness.

"If I have to lose weight," he asked, "how about jogging? I hear that will take care of it."

"You don't have to jog," I said. "You can lose weight sitting down."

It is my considered opinion that treating obesity is one of the most important of all methods to find fitness. If you can maintain normal weight—and you can do so without jogging—you have built the foundation for good health.

Since the treatment of obesity is so urgent and important, I'll show

115

you how to neutralize many of the obstacles to its elimination. I'll offer you strategies for weight control. I'll also list some tactics you can use in completely overcoming obesity. Above all, I want you to know you can do all this without lifting a finger, or foot, in exercise.

Stratagem 1
Prevention of Adiposity Easier than Treatment

Approximately 80 million Americans are overweight to some degree. Some are actually fat, others are pleasingly plump, and still others only a few pounds over.

If you are a member of the latter group, pay attention to this dictum: it's easier to prevent excess weight than to take it off.

The most important weapon in the arsenal of prevention is awareness. When was the last time you stepped on the platform of a scale? Did you disregard any evidence that you had put on a few pounds during the past year or years?

This is the crucial point. Blissfully putting small weight gains out of your mind is the sure first step toward chronic obesity. Taking active steps to counteract your enemy while it is still only a minor threat is the surest way to stay slim.

The scale is not the only warning system. What has your mirror been telling you lately? What have your friends been saying? Perhaps the best of all warning systems is the fit, or misfit, of your clothes. What greater shock than not to be able to get into a favorite dress or suit?

What have you determined to do about it, if anything? Perhaps you have resorted to rationalization? It all began when I gave up cigarettes. I guess it runs in my family. Pounds began to pile on after my gall bladder operation. I guess my trouble is that I don't exercise enough.

Awareness, not rationalization, is the answer to the conquest of beginning obesity. Face up to whatever your mirror tells you. Face up to what your friends tell you. Face up to what your ill-fitting clothes tell you. Then it will become natural to ask yourself where the extra pounds are coming from. Have I become a nibbler? Do I overeat at the table? Too many sweets? Not getting sufficient exercise? Seek and ye shall find.

Samuel Johnson said, "Abstinence for me is easier than temperance." This can also apply to the prevention of obesity. You will more easily hold off those extra pounds if you can entirely abstain from the following, or at least only "taste" them: Syrups, sugar, sweetened drinks, honey, marmalade, jellies and jams, cookies, cakes and pies, salad oils, fried foods, nuts, olives, chocolate, cream, candies and ice cream.

However, do not become too conscious of the scale. I have known patients who were drawn like a magnet to the scale half a dozen time a day. For some, nightly weigh-ins are necessary. Others become aware they must curtail their gains after weekly weigh-ins.

Another essential element of the stratagem of prevention is to realize that taking short cuts instead of curtailing extra calories is a shorter cut to defeat. Even if the weight loss is a little slower, it is better to achieve it without such temporary crutches as drugs that promote a feeling of well-being; medicines that reduce appetite; stimulants that increase metabolism—thryoid extract; tranquilizers, sedatives, and sleeping pills to get you over some rough spots while dieting; an excess of bulky foods, vegetables and fruits, which may produce intestinal irritation; diuretics to eliminate excess fluids; and, last but not least, jogging for miles in hopes such exertion will nullify bad habits in eating. At times, under strict supervision, there may be a place for such temporary crutches in recovering from obesity. But remember that such therapy should not be of the machine-gun hit-or-miss variety.

Of all the elements in your campaign to lose weight, your awareness, will power, and good motivation are perhaps the most essential. Envision yourself slim, as already having conquered obesity. Consider the motto of President Paul Meyer of Success Motivation, Inc.: "Whatever you vividly imagine, ardently desire, sincerely believe, and enthusiastically act upon—must inevitably come to pass."

Borrow this successful businessman's credo in your fight against obesity. Repeat it daily. It is an effective weapon. It will help insure victory in melting off those excess pounds.

Stratagem 2
Psychology of Obesity

If you are overweight, it is likely that you have psychological problems. These may be major or minor. They depend not only on the degree of your obesity, but on your individual reaction to your social environment. The question remains, which came first, the proverbial chicken or the egg?

For example, consider what Dr. Walter Menninger has said:

> But excessive eating also has roots in our emotions. The child relates to the world entirely with his mouth: everything goes into it—nipple, pacifier, fist, thumb, toys. All through life we get pleasure using our mouth—eating, chewing, sucking, drinking, smoking, talking, gossiping, kissing.
>
> A delicious meal should satisfy most anyone. But some people consistently take in more food than they need, as if to make up for a deficiency in pleasure and satisfaction from some other body activity. . . . Some will overeat and gain weight as a substitute for love or to make up for the loss of a loved one. . . . Some substitute excessive eating for sexual pleasure. . . . Some people use overeating to compensate for or reduce rage and inner resentment about a frustration or disappointment. . . . People keep looking for the easy solution—the diet, which suggests you can eat as much as you want and still lose weight.

Mark this page. Return to it daily while you are in the process of melting off your extra poundage, especially if you have been tempted to engage in jogging to fight your obesity. Reread and digest its underlying philosophy of the psychology of weight gain and weight loss. Understanding it will help you win in the battle of the bulge.

It is true that emotional imbalance often creates obesity. However, in some patients, the psychological problems do not arise until after the weight has been gained. Miss E, a young, unmarried school teacher, is sad. She suffers a guilt complex, lives in anxiety, feels shame and inferiority when among her peers. She has gained twenty-five pounds during the school term. Ah, you say, naturally she feels as she does; she is fat. She looks at other slim teachers and feels an inner resentment at herself for allowing herself to gain. All this has added up to an emotional imbalance which has caused her to nibble constantly.

However, my experience tells me that the relationship between obesity and emotional problems doesn't always produce a pat answer for the cause of weight gain. Ask this teacher whether she had these psychological problems before or after she gained weight. She may answer that she considered herself a stable person, in good emotional equilibrium. "I don't know why I have gained," she'd explain. "I guess I just got into the habit of nibbling because I learned to enjoy snacks. I didn't begin to feel nervous, depressed, and shameful until after the added pounds made a mess of my appearance."

Simple explanation? In her case, yes. But not always so. Many obese patients have told me that their emotional imbalance came before their obesity. They pointed the finger directly at their nervousness as the reason for overloading calories.

Whether symptoms come before or after weight production, one thing has now been evident for some time: the fat man, woman, or child is not invariably the happy person. The outer facade—a smiling face—more often conceals an inner pain.

An essential stratagem to employ is to keep reinforcing the truth that your body's requirements for energy are usually less after you turn 30 and still less after 40. Your metabolism slows down as you become older; you need fewer calories to maintain your normal weight. If your eating habits remain the same and your physical activities lessen, you can understand why obesity takes command.

If you remind yourself of these basic facts you will be more than one up in your daily bout against excessive weight. Mind and matter can be enemies or friends; much depends upon the psychology you develop in losing weight.

Stratagem 3
Motivation

People of normal weight look on obesity as a joke. Never having had to do battle with calories, they think that the difficulty of this problem is exaggerated. Blessed with the ability to eat whatever they wish without becoming fat, they do not realize how much this problem disrupts the lives of so many. Listen to this unhappy mother:

> You will probably read this and have a good laugh. Then you will throw it away. But please help! I'm tired of trying to lose weight. I'm medium build and weigh over 175 pounds. I've tried diet pills, shots, fad diets, doctors' diets. For one month I even tried jogging until I developed a bad knee. Then I turned to diet clubs. The first time I lost 19½ pounds; you win a trophy when you lose 20 pounds. Well, I lost that trophy by a half a pound. Then I regained those 19½ pounds and added 8 more.
>
> I hate being fat. I've been trying to lose weight since I was 13. I weighed 175 pounds then. I went to a doctor and lost 30 pounds. Now, at 26, I've lost over a thousand pounds altogether. I'm married and have two children. My husband tells me I am fat, then he turns around and buys me candy! I get very depressed about being fat. So I eat to feel better. It is a vicious circle. Help! I make jokes and say, "I can't wait until I'm a grandmother so I can eat and be fat in comfort."
>
> Why can't I keep the weight off? Life doesn't seem worth living any more. If I had all the money I've spent trying to lose weight, I could buy a new home. Besides, my husband is getting disgusted with me. What can I do?

I told her that her problem, like that of many others who are overweight, is a stubborn one. The solution narrows down to one word: motivation. Without achieving the proper motivation, the chronically obese person continues to flounder around helplessly in a sea of calories for the remainder of his or her life.

What do I mean by proper motivation? You will have to ask yourself just why you want to lose. To save your marriage? To improve your health? For appearance? To overcome your depression? Seek and you will discover a real hard-core reason that will give you the will to look straight at the most tempting dishes and treats, and toss them away uneaten.

This is only one important aspect of successful weight reduction. There are, of course, others. But accept this stratagem for what it is worth: without real, honest-to-goodness motivation to lose, your weight problem will stay with you forever. Harsh? Nevertheless, true.

Once I asked a famous architect what was his greatest creation. Not immodestly he said, "me! Taking off 75 pounds about 20 years ago and keeping them off."

Stratagem 4
Overcoming Boredom

Boredom is the handmaiden of obesity. When you are bored, you wonder what to do next. As if in a dream, you may discover yourself standing in front of your refrigerator.

Without hesitation, you turn the handle, swing the door, and begin an inspection of the shelves. Oral satisfaction is the temporary antidote for boredom. Satisfying your hunger pains is not a part of it. Boredom itself is sufficient excuse for a raid on the ice box.

It's a standing joke that for the TV watcher, the commercial break, which is supposedly boring, is the proper time for taking a tidbit out of the refrigerator or pantry. Whether it's a slice of ham or cheese, some leftover cake, cookies, ice cream, a handful of peanuts or potato chips, a few chocolates, a can of beer, such are the ways boredom invites the intake of extra calories—and extra poundage.

Boredom comes in all sizes and guises. Eating frankfurters or peanuts at a baseball game may be one indication, although you may seem actively interested in the proceedings. The trouble is that you are only passively involved in the game.

To forestall boredom learn to become an active participant in daily spheres of action. Much depends on your dedication to the job you are doing. If you are busy, active, and deeply interested, you will rarely think of food. However, if your job bores you, it is likely you will be the one who takes coffee breaks more often and fills up on snatches of food.

It is not only at work that you should protect yourself against boredom. Be on your guard at home. It is here that one should avoid "doing nothing but sitting around" with food. The strategem is to learn to fill these voids and gaps with interesting, absorbing hobbies: reading, writing, listening to music, playing chess or other games, or finding work to do inside and outside the house.

Idle hands and brain usually end up thinking of food and shoving it (or dropping it daintily) into the oral cavity. When this becomes a habit pattern it is an open invitation to obesity.

Stratagem 5
Big Breakfast

I have misplaced the name of the author of the following quotation: "Eat like a king in the morning, a prince for lunch, and pauper for dinner." It makes good sense. Yet, so many take breakfast on the run—a cup of black coffee or worse, still, nothing at all.

I know many joggers who can find time to run only in the morning before work and who consequently go without breakfast and often without lunch. Then they wonder why they don't lose weight. After a heavy dinner, they walk carelessly in a no-man's-island filled with many booby traps and hidden caloric mines. Then come the tidbits that fill the TV commercial voids, the unconscious tread of slippered feet to the kitchen, the temptations behind pantry doors and refrigerator shelves—all beckoning to the hungry fellow or girl to add more snacks to the daily caloric intake. Such are the enemies, the little gremlins, that pile excess weight on unsuspecting innocents like ourselves.

I have believed for years that a big breakfast is good. To put it more simply: break down the word breakfast and we get 'break (the) fast.' Consider how many hours have passed between an early dinner and breakfast on the following day. When children leave for school on empty stomachs and businessmen or women leave for the office hungry, efficiency and energy output is bound to fall below normal standards. More important, they save their hunger and overeat in the evening and become obese.

Six small meals a day is the soundest eating program for the physiology. If one prefers three meals a day, it is advisable to reconstruct habits. Some say they can't eat anything at all for breakfast because they can't even face food in the morning without getting queasy. Many more, I believe, skip breakfast because of time limitations. A good strategy is to get up at least a half hour earlier. This allows for relaxed transition from sleep to wakefulness. An absence of tension invites a larger breakfast.

Instead of taking a cup of coffee or nothing at all, you will learn to enjoy fruit, cereal, eggs, ham or bacon, toast, and coffee. Some other mornings, hot cakes and sausage may be your choice. For lunch, have a fruit salad, a glass of skimmed milk, and crackers. For dinner, have toast, vegetables, salad, soup, fish, fowl, or meat. If you take a highball or martini before dinner, have no dessert. Learn to swap one for the other.

Enjoying a big breakfast is worthy of the name "stratagem." Try it and see if it doesn't work.

Stratagem 6
Overcoming Risk Factors in Coronary Disease

"Why is there so much written about the dangers of obesity and coronary disease? I think that the American Heart Association is scaring more people than helping them—like the American Cancer Society, for example. Don't you agree?"

It's evident that you don't realize that prevention is more important than cure. When there isn't a fire, you don't have to put it out. It's likely that no member of your immediate family has ever been threatened by or died from coronary heart disease. Otherwise, you would not be so complacent about it. You would be more likely to respect the long columns of statistics which add up to many thousands of premature deaths from heart attacks that might have been prevented.

Obesity and coronary disease are major health problems not only in the United States, but in many other countries as well. In 1970 some 666,000 Americans died of coronary disease. What is increasingly disturbing is that many young Americans are disabled or killed by coronary disease. It is no longer an old man's disease.

Therefore, I agree with the American Heart Association that there is still room for widespread dissemination of information about coronary disease. It is surprising how many are still completely unaware of its dangers—and how to combat it. And it is because of the increasing susceptibility of younger people to heart attacks that I have been warning jogging enthusiasts who reach the age of 35 to have complete heart checkups that include stress testing of the heart before engaging in exercise. Too many under 40 who jog believe they are safe simply because they are young.

I have said earlier that there are many risk factors in coronary disease. A good strategy is to recognize the dangers and then try to neutralize them. If you weigh too much, you'd better lose. If you smoke, quit. If your blood pressure is higher than normal, treat it. If you have diabetes or gout, bring it under control. If you are tense, learn to relax. If your cholesterol and triglycerides are too high, follow a special diet and be attentive to other recommendations by your physician. If you are physically inactive, get into the habit of taking walks daily. Jogging is not the only alternative.

I tell people not to be exasperated by all the warnings that are being spread around, but to be thankful for them. The best way to fight coronary heart disease is to face it head on. One of the best ways to prevent atherosclerosis (the arterial degeneration that is the precursor of coronary disease) is to keep your weight normal. When that happens, we will not keep on scaring you as much as we have in the past.

Strategem 7
Expect Your Doctor to Offer Specific Advice

My husband is eating himself to death. I think the trouble began when he went to our doctor two years ago. He asked if it would be all right to take a banana split or chocolate malted once in a while.

The doctor said, "Of course, you may have them once in a

while." Since then my husband has put on about fifty pounds. He is only in his late 30s, but is already beginning to look like a man in his late fifties. My husband's idea of "once in a while" is a few malteds a day and at least a pint of rich ice cream before he goes to bed. Don't you think the doctor should have given him more specific warnings?

Just as children tire of hearing their parents say, "Don't do this" and "Don't do that," adult patients begin to rebel at their doctor's restrictions. They will smoke and drink or overexercise in spite of warnings from the doctor.

But there is another side to it. Often the doctor isn't specific enough. When he says, "You can drink a little," the patient often changes the "little" to "too much." If he says "One or two cigarettes aren't harmful," he opens the door to the patient who is aching to go on a smoking binge.

And of course this is also true when the problem is overeating. The patient will take advantage of nonspecific advice. Lack of communication is what throws the proverbial monkey wrench into the machinery of everyday living.

It is a good strategy for you to know exactly what your doctor means before leaving his office. We know that cigarettes are health threats. Therefore, it is our job to say, "Better not smoke at all." If we know that you are on the borderline between social drinking and actual chronic alcoholism, we should say "Better quit entirely." You should be told directly, without any equivocation. Otherwise, you may return home and say, "The doctor said it is all right for me to take a drink once in a while" or "eat as much as I want within reason."

If you understand exactly what the doctor means, the responsibility becomes your own. This is as true for dieting as it is for the control of any bad habit that is potentially harmful.

Stratagem 8
Eat Less, Chew More

It's not only what you eat that is so important; it's how much you eat—and how often. Calories do count, but how you dispose of them is an important factor in the dietary problem.

If you have diabetes, of course it matters what you eat, as it does if you have pernicious anemia or any other condition that may require a specific dietary intake. But for most of us who are apparently healthy, the habit of eating becomes important.

Occasionally, I receive common sense hints from patients on the art of eating. One said: "I have the secret of good health. Most people eat too fast and too much. Here's what helped me keep healthy to the age of 75: eat less; chew more."

Another confided that "the trouble with most people is that when the clock says it's time to eat, they take food whether or not they are hungry. The secret of good health is to miss a meal when you don't feel like eating. Nature has told dogs how to take care of themselves. Many times your pet will refuse appetizing food and skip a meal until he really feels like eating. Take a lesson from your dog."

Still another patient suggested that it's best never to eat unless you are happy and relaxed. "I'm 81," he said, "and have found this is important for good health. I always forego food whenever I am tense and worried. I don't let it curdle in my stomach. Of course, a nip of brandy or a glass of sherry before eating helps take away the tense feeling. But if in any doubt, it's better to wait until the stomach untwists itself. Or, better still, forego eating entirely until the next time."

All these are excellent suggestions. They are practical and prevent indigestion or worse. Remember also that the large meal that overloads the stomach also overloads the circulation. Don't burden your heart and arteries unnecessarily. According to some studies, a heavy meal adds about 30 percent to the work of the heart. This is one reason why patients with angina pectoris have more frequent attacks of chest pain if they exert directly after a meal. Other studies have shown that animals fed five or six small meals a day are healthier and thinner than those fed one extralarge meal.

Stratagem 9
Using Your Appetite as an Ally

This is the stratagem of stratagems. Let me tell you how a good friend used his appetite as an ally rather than encountering it as an enemy day after day. He thus outwitted his enemy, obesity. This method of attack has also worked as well with hundreds of others who were willing to adhere to it faithfully.

My friend was completely discouraged. He had tried diet after diet, but had failed. Weighing 275 pounds, he was an attractive, extremely intelligent personality buried in unattractive mounds of fat.

"What shall I do?" he asked. "I'm only 38. I know I'm shortening my life expectancy. But I have this strong urge to eat things I shouldn't, especially at night: ice cream—at least a pint every night while I watch TV—pies, cookies, baloney sandwiches, beer, sweet drinks. Is there any wonder or mystery where all the excess weight comes from? Of course not. But I'll make this confession. I'm willing to give reduction one more try if you can come up with a method I'll accept. Can you?"

Right then and there I had this sudden flash of insight. I said, "Why not make a friend out of your appetite rather than treat it as an enemy? Most dieters like yourself are in a constant struggle with this strong force called "appetite." Why struggle? Show your friendliness. Be thankful you have an appetite, but don't overstep the bounds of friendship. Partaking of the foods, fattening or otherwise, that your appetite desires, but in a special way.

"The trick is to taste foods you especially like. Never say no to the most fattening. For example, you have been in the habit of taking a pint of ice cream at night. Don't quit entirely. Take a spoonful. Then quit. A piece of pie? Don't quit entirely. Take a forkful. And so on. A sweet drink? Take one swallow.

"You will note this is a psychological attack on the enemy, making him a friend. You haven't denied him his taste of food or drink. All you have done is limit the intake. In this way you satisfy your tastebuds—even though your stomach rebels at first.

"Simple? Too ridiculously simple? Yes. But so was the discovery of the law of gravity. Try it, my friend."

Within one year he lost 100 pounds, and for the rest of his life he has weighed no more than 175 pounds.

"It has been easy," he said. "It's a wonderful way to keep trim and fit. Never insult your appetite and you have an ally for life. Give him a lick or a sip—and quit. He remains ever grateful for your consideration. After a while you can come to a dead stop after applying the brakes—without screeching.

"My appetite now accepts the fact that both of us should refrain from filling up on fattening foods. We sit down to our regular meals taking enough of what we need, and we do not go in search for the sweets and fats that will fatten us up again.

So this is the basic secret of dieting: not dieting—never disallowing the tastebuds in your tongue and mouth the relish of at least a taste of whatever food or drink you crave, not denying, but tasting the forbidden; learning to be satisfied with a morsel, not a mouthful. If you have learned to be both friend and master of your appetite, you will no longer be victimized by the many fad diets that keep sprouting up month after month, year after year.

Such no-nonsense weight control offers the surest antidote for excess weight. You need not become a student of food content and caloric equivalents. You need not develop a willpower of steel to resist accumulating weight. All you need to do is be yourself. Don't strain to accomplish weight loss. Easy does it. Just learn to taste and not indulge in forbidden fruit.

Everyone is looking for instant weightlessness. Don't be in a hurry to lose. Don't fuss with special recipes or exercises.

When I have, in the past, revealed my taste formula for weight reduction, many patients at first have shown disappointment, as people do when a magician explains how he performed a puzzling trick. They like to consider dieting a mystery. However, when pounds had dissolved months later, they became believers. This method is the answer to the search for a sure cure for obesity.

TACTICS

Remember that weight control is a war—with yourself. Each day you engage in a battle with your apprently benign foe, obesity. He uses dirty tricks to entice you to overeat. Your only hope is to neutralize his efforts. Counterattack with tactics of your own.

I have already given you stratagems that will help you overcome obesity. Now I offer TACTICS that will reinforce your will to keep your weight normal. Using them to control your weight, you will have no need for such extracurricular activities as jogging to keep fit. If you are not overweight, your ordinary daily physical activities will supply all the exercise you need to keep healthy and fit. Remember that control of obesity is the antidote for jogging.

• There is no more certain way to ensure longevity than by the simple method of maintaining a normal weight. Sir Francis Bacon tells of the reply of an old man who gave this reason for his long life: "I always ate before I was hungry and drank before I was dry. Following this rule, I was sure never to eat nor drink much at a time."

• Dieting is not a mysterious trick only your doctor knows. You can learn to perform it yourself.

• Ask yourself, "Would I be willing to go through life with a forty-pound bag of potatoes strapped to my back? Would I mind toting it around to the theater, my office, the golf course, or a dance? And even while I sleep?" Unlikely. Yet, it is even more unseemly to allow forty pounds of extra fat droplets to infiltrate every organ of your body.

• Your first weapon is the realization that obesity is stealthy. It is especially dangerous because it invades without pain. It is a friendly sort of enemy.

• Accept the fact that so-called special diets are not devastating weapons against obesity.

• Dieting should become an easily bearable, long-term habit. It should not be a violent, painful deprivation.

• Keep your dieting to yourself. It must be a secret resolve. When you talk about it to your friends, inevitably you release and lose a major force of your original resolution.

• When you lose your excess weight, prepare for a resurgence of vitality, a lifting of your spirits, and renewed eagerness for living. Do not allow this euphoria to lower your guard against obesity.

• Keep reminding yourself that the important question is not just how you look outside or how your clothes fit. What is more essential is how you look inside, the effect of excess fat on your arteries, blood pressure, and heart.

• The cheapest and easiest premium for good health and good

looks is the development of the will to lose. You will lose weight if you can convince yourself that it has become the strongest desire in your life.

• Don't keep looking for a traitor in the ranks if you fail to lose. The fat man with a tight collar often blames the laundry, not the bakery.

• Nibbling may be more avantagious than taking regular meals, but nibblers may be overeaters, too.

• When you are fat you carry excess baggage loaded with dynamite. Your doctor cannot predict if or when you may blow up, but he knows it's more likely that you will than will your slim neighbor.

• As a man, do you try to hide your potbelly behind a double-breasted suit? As a woman, do you sigh in disappointment when you look at the slim models display the new spring and fall styles?

• It's still possible to eat, drink, and be merry—if you will take the first two in moderation.

• The cure for obesity comes down to one word: moderation.

• You can be fit and 40, but not fit, fat, and 40.

• Socrates said, "Bad men live that they may eat and drink, whereas good men eat and drink that they may live."

• Dieting should not be sporadic—on and off the calorie wagon. Self-denial for six days and a Roman holiday on the seventh is unproductive of good results.

• Females are more prone to obesity. This may be due to added glandular adjustments: the extra globules of fat wait to invade at such times as puberty, after marriage and childbirth, after lactation, and during menopause.

• Most people who decide to go on a diet make only a superficial effort to do so, instead of dedicating themselves to the battle.

• Beware of the ways extra calories inflitrate: dinner celebrations, cocktail parties, weddings, bachelor parties, meetings, bridge clubs, poker games, cruises, auto trips and vacations. The "American Plan" at hotels beckons added poundage.

• Learn to pass by your refrigerator door, especially during TV commercials.

• Each to his own poisons: one becomes a chain smoker, another an alcoholic, still another obese. Some succumb to all three. Alcoholism is a major problem all by itself. Have you resolved both to give up smoking and to go on a diet at the same time? This is usually a superhuman effort. Try giving up tobacco first. Then concentrate your attack on obesity.

• Frequent coffee breaks—with snacks—are one of obesity's dirty tricks.

• Obesity involves emotions: divorce, loss of a loved one, loss of a job, fear of illness. Such are reasons why some overeat. Food acts as a tranquilizer for those filled with tension and stress.

• Your diet can follow you anywhere, anytime. Therefore it's your responsibility to make no excuses. You must be alert all the time: weekdays, weekends, workdays, holidays, and social celebrations.

• Learn how to say "no, thank you" to the hostess at dinner.

• Don't rely on steam baths, massage, rubber suits, special injections, diuretics, appetite suppressors, and exercise to successfully counteract slips of diet.

• Don't be disappointed and discouraged if dieting doesn't cause weight loss in "that special place". There is no known way to shoot the green arrow of weight loss to special areas of the body for spot reduction, but it's the rule that when weight decreases, so do inches and size.

• Practical tips: Use small plates. Don't be a plate cleaner. Eat slowly, putting down the fork after every second forkful. (Eighty to 90 percent of the obese are fast eaters.) Don't dally at the table, munching leftovers.

• Here are ten bad habits that lessen the chances of good health and longevity: (1) abnormal daily stresses and tension in the home and at work, (2) self-treatment and procrastination, (3) smoking, (4) overdrinking, (5) undervacationing, (6) undersleeping, (7) resentment, (8) worry unnecessarily, (9) overworking, and (10) overeating.

• Look about you on the streets. You will note that with few exceptions most men and women over 70 are thin. When a fat one comes puffing along it's likely St. Peter was looking the other way.

• Excess weight is slow poison. It deadens heart power. A full stomach adds about 30 percent more load to the heart's work.

• Much of the harm of the word "diet" must be undone. We have placed it on too high a pedestal. We have made a fetish of it.

• Many are worldly wise but pound-foolish.

• A calorie is the quantity of heat required to raise the temperature of one kilogram of water one degree centigrade.

• In your pursuit of weight loss, have a daily goal instead of a yearly goal. Otherwise the trip will seem too long and arduous to accomplish.

• All patients with obesity do not have hypothyroidism, yet many with normal basal metabolisms begin to lose stubborn pounds with the help of measured amounts of thyroid extract.

• More people who are fat have high cholesterol levels, yet when they lose weight, their cholesterol often falls without medication.

• Don't rely on exercise for weight loss. You'd have to walk forty or more miles to burn off one pound of fat.

• Try a bit of chocolate before dinner. For some this spoils the appetite.

Some common offenders are one hamburger on a bun, eight ounces of beer, a chocolate-nut sundae with whipped cream (about 1,000 calories), three martinis and ten almonds (600 calories), and an average serving of applie pie and 1½ ounces of cheese (1,000 calories). Beware also of bread, potatoes, spaghetti, macaroni, cake, ice cream, candy, sodas, pies, nuts, fried foods, fatty meats, butter, oily dressings, heavy cream, cocktails, and beer.

Other foods to shun are ham, pork, bacon, frankfurters, duck, corned beef, fish packed in oil, and delicatessen products. Avoid grapes, canned fruits, dates, olives, raisins, figs, jellies, or jams. Don't dally at the table with breadsticks, crackers, or Danish, French, or Italian breads or rolls. Sorry no pizzas, doughnuts, or hot bisuits. Birthday cake? Who is to say no to that?

The starving may have lean meat, poultry, and liver without flour, thick sauces, or bread crumbs. Also permitted are fish, boiled or steamed; eggs, boiled or poached; and potatoes, boiled, baked in skins, or steamed, but not fried, roasted, sauteed, or French fried. Vegetables of all kinds, fresh or canned, maybe cooked in any way except with fat. Salads and tomatoes are fine, but without oil or mayonnaise. All fresh fruits are fine in moderation, as are clear soups. You may have salt, pepper, vinegar, and mustard. Use saccharin for sweetening, and have a glass of milk daily as well as three small pieces of bread. Cole slaw is acceptable if it is made without mayonnaise; use lemon, vinegar, or tomato juice for salad dressings.

Too many people live on lopsided diets. According to psychologist Paul A. Fine, "The average American lives on a diet of Oreos, peanut butter, Crisco, TV dinners, cake mix, macaroni and cheese, Pepsi and Coke, pizzas, Jell-o, hamburgers, Rice-a-Roni, Spaghetto-os, pork and beans, Heinz ketchup, and instant coffee." As a result many have deficiencies of essential vitamins, minerals, and proteins—and many are obese. According to Dr. George Christakis of New York, "About two-thirds of the nation's chronic disease and public health problems are nutrition related." As Albert Stunkard, psychiatrist, declared, "Overweight is very likely the greatest preventable cause of death in the United States."

I have given you stratagems and tactics in detail. One or more may be sufficient to set you in the right direction of maintaining proper weight. Do not be overwhelmed by the seemingly endless directions for being slim. My purpose has been to cut your obesity down to size. Are you ready for a new fitting? Then don't let procrastination be your undoing again. You don't start to stop smoking tomorrow. You don't start to stop drinking tomorrow. You can't start stop-overeating tomorrow. That's too late. Start today.

If you are physically lazy, it's your chief recourse for fitness. Lie in your hammock or sit in your rocking chair at a normal weight, and you're in as good health or better than the joggers who pass by looking at you in derision, but secretely envious of your ability to relax.

In *Save Your Stomach* (Crown Publishers, N.Y., 1977) Lawrence Galton writes, "But the view that lack of exercise is responsible for obesity, common though it is, seems quite vulnerable to some investigators." He then quotes Surgeon-Captain T. L. Cleaves, former director of medical research at the Institute of Naval Medicine in Britain: "The sole cause of obesity, Cleaves is convinced, lies in the consumption of refined carbohydrates, and neither a large appetite nor a dislike of exercise is a cause."

9

PROPER BREATHING: THE ESSENTIAL EXERCISE

In *Rock Wagram,* William Saroyan wrote: "The only thing a man does all his life is breathe. The instant he inhales he is alive, the instant he exhales, but does not inhale again, he is dead.

"A man is very nearly everything the first time he inhales, he is very nearly nothing the last time he exhales, but between the first inhale and the last exhale a man is many things."

It may seem ironic that I should prescribe a system of exercises for the diaphragm in a book in which I appear to denigrate exercise of any kind. But I believe it is essential that you be aware that the heart is not the sole muscle on which you depend for survival. Too often overlooked is the need to keep in trim the muscle called the diaphragm.

To call exercise something that can be done "standing, sitting or lying down" is a misnomer. Instead, let's call it "lazy conditioning." After you read my recommendations I think you will agree that the procedures I outline for diaphragmatic-fitness are not in the same category of energy-expenditure produced by jogging.

When your diaphragm is fully-powered it is more likely that your heart will be able to dispatch well-oxygenated blood to every cell in your body. The efficiency of liver, kidneys, and of the heart itself (through its coronary blood supply) depend upon it.

If your heart is a pump and your arteries the pipes, then your lungs are the bellows. You cannot be fit and healthy unless you know how to breathe. Forgetting about fitness, you can't even remain alive if you lack oxygen for as little as four or six minutes. Your brain's appetite is continuous. It's evident, therefore, that your existence depends on your maintaining the proper exchange between oxygen and carbon dioxide. This takes place in the lungs.

Air is inspired through your nose and mouth; then it slips down into two large branches called bronchi, one entering the right lung, the other the left. The bronchi inside the lungs keep subdividing into smaller bronchioles, and these end in millions of thin-walled sacs called alveoli. Each of these is in contact with tiny blood vessels called capillaries, where the oxygen-carbon dioxide exchange takes place. Oxygen is then taken up by hemaglobin and distributed throughout the body, and carbon dioxide (CO_2) is diffused through the nose.

The lungs consist of a spongy tissue and are united by the windpipe. Between them lie the heart, gullet, larger blood vessels, lymph nodes, and nerves. The membranous sac called the pleura, which lines the lungs, secrets lubricating fluid that prevents friction as the lungs expand and contract. Each lung contains an estimated 375 million air sacs or alveoli.

A man's lungs weigh 3½ pounds, a woman's 2¾ pounds. The total air volume the lungs can hold varies. It ranges from 3 to 5 quarts (3,000 to 5,000 cubic centimeters). This total is called the vital capacity. During ordinary breathing, the amount of air that passes in and out is about 500 cc. This is called the tidal air. After you have completed an ordinary expiration, you can forcibly breathe in about 3,000 cc of air. This is called the complemental air.

When your lungs come to rest after ordinary expiration you can force out about 1,000 cc of air, the so-called supplemental air. This is reserve air, which remains in your lungs during ordinary breathing. No matter how hard you blow out, there always remains about 1,000 to 1,500 cc of residual air.

During ordinary breathing, you use only about one-fourth of your lung capacity. A large portion of the lungs do not receive fresh air each time you breathe. This is why the periodic deep breathing I will describe is so valuable.

The most important muscle in breathing is the diaphragm. This is the large, dome-shaped muscle that separates the abdomen from the chest. When you take a deep inspiration, this muscle moves downward and become flattened, increasing the space in the chest. At the same time, the small muscles attached to your ribs also move the chest upward. When you let air out, the flattened diaphragm curves up into your chest again, your ribs move inward, and air leaves the lungs.

The diaphragm has another important function. It helps to support you. If you want to lift a heavy suitcase or move a piano, you will unconsciously take a deep breath, contracting your diaphragm and fixing it. Since the diaphragm is attached to the ribs, it helps hold them in position as you exert.

Your lungs themselves don't actively expand and contract. Movements of your chest cavity control them. When the cavity expands, your lungs expand to fill them. This lowers the air pressure in the lungs, which causes air to be drawn down the windpipe. During expiration, the opposite happens. It's the CO_2 left in the blood that stimulates the respiratory center in the brain.

Your lungs are never completely squeezed out. Usual breathing takes in only about one-eighth of what can be inhaled and exhaled by deep breathing. This is not as wasteful as you may believe. If you completely emptied your lungs each time, you'd be living from one breath to the next.

THE NEED FOR BREATHING EXERCISES

The chances are that you underbreathe. Whether you are healthy or ill, you will obtain an increased measure of vitality by breathing correctly.

When was the last time you consciously took a number of successive, deep breaths? Probably not in months or years. And if you did, just how did you breathe? By proper belly-breathing, or improperly by forcibly raising your shoulders and chest? The brilliant and famous chest specialist, Alvan L. Barach, M.D. told me: "The change from an upper thoracic to a predominently diaphragmatic respiration is the single, most valuable contribution of the various physiologic methods employed to improve the mechanics of breathing."

Learn how to breathe with your diaphragm and you overcome lazy breathing. You'll get more air into your lungs. With your doctor's permission, practice one or more of the following exercises fifteen to thirty minutes a day. They are about the only conscious exercise you will need to find the fitness you seek.

Exercise 1

Learn to exercise your diaphragm without jogging. You can do so while lying down, sitting, or standing. The key is to use your diaphragm rather than your chest to breathe properly.

Watch your navel as your belly goes in and out. When you breathe in, your belly goes out; when you breathe out, your belly goes in.

Do this basic exercise for 3 minutes, twice a day during the first two weeks; then for three minutes, once a day the second week. Place palms of your hands over your upper abdomen to feel your diaphragm work.

Following a month of such practice you will discover that belly breathing has become a habit. You can vary this exercise by doing it in different positions—sitting, standing, or lying down.

Exercise 2

In normal breathing you take in about a pint of air and let out the same amount. This is shallow breathing. You must learn how to expel the foul air—how to exhale. The amount of fresh air you inhale depends on how much you have pushed out.

A descriptive name for this exercise is "silent-whistle" or "pursed-lip" breathing. You let out your breath normally. Then you purse your lips as if to whistle and keep forcing air out until you feel your diaphragm is as far up as it will go. Having expelled the air, you then take as deep a breath as possible through your nose bellowing out the diaphragm. Then let the air out gently, without forcing it.

Repeat three times in a row, three times a day. This type of breathing, repeated so many times in succession is all right provided you don't get dizzy or have palpitation, nervousness, or light-headedness. These are symptoms of hyperventilation, which comes about with the loss of too much carbon dioxide.

If you perform this exercise standing, bend your head and trunk forward. When you perform it sitting, bend your trunk farther and farther forward until you feel you've squeezed out as much air as possible. When you do it lying down, as you begin your pursed-lip expiration bend your knees, pull up your thighs as far as they will go. When no more air seems remaining, straighten your legs and inspire quickly using diaphragmatic action.

Using this silent-whistle exercise routinely, you will feel fit and buoyant. It clears your mind quickly after sleep or a nap, and it promotes relaxation at bedtime.

Exercise 3

To help strengthen your diaphragm, buy a "breathing bag" at a health store, or make a zippered canvas bag large enough to hold ten to twenty-five pounds of clean sand or buck shot. Begin with ten pounds.

Before bedtime lie on the floor or on a firm mattress. Support your head on a comfortable pillow. Elevate your supported legs to a fifteen or twenty degree angle. Place the bag on the mid to lower part of your abdomen for 15 minutes. Make no special effort to breathe. At the end of three months you will be able to tolerate a weight of twenty-five pounds.

Exercise 4

Learn to nap, head down on a slant board, tilted at about fifteen degrees. Breathe quietly. This is refreshing relaxation.

Exercise 5

Take a deep breath. Hold it fifteen to thirty seconds. Then let it out with a rush. Exhale with your lips pursed for a more complete expulsion. Repeat two or three times a day. Don't use this overbreathing technique before swimming or diving. You may get into serious breathing difficulty.

Exercise 6

Buy twelve four-pound paper bags. If they don't fit comfortably around the mouth and nose, use six-pound bags instead. Fit the edges of a bag tightly around your face. Be sure no air escapes when you expel air into bag. The purpose is to build up carbon dioxide and rebreathe it. Inhale and exhale into the bag with mouth open.

Perform this exercise for five minutes one to three times a day. This exercise is excellent for helping to overcome anxiety, but don't use it without your doctor's consent.

Keep remembering that breathing is normally an unconscious process. My purpose is to make you occasionally conscious of your breathing, but not abnormally so. Remind yourself that these are simply exercises. Their purpose is to strengthen the force of your diaphragm, make your breathing more efficient, and increase the available oxygen. You will soon know which are more effective and how much time you need to spend. A stop watch will help.

Here is a practical test that will show you the effect of your breathing exercises on your lung capacity. Count off one hundred words in any book before you begin the test. Take a deep breath, stop watch in hand, and read as far as you can without taking another breath. Speak the words in normal tones, not stopping for punctuation marks.

In the beginning you may get only as far as thirty to fifty words. Within a week or two after your breathing exercises have begun, you will easily get as far as one hundred words after one deep breath, and each will be distinctly and easily spoken.

Awareness of the need to keep your diaphragm fit and in good tone is especially important if your way of life does not include jogging or other physical exertions.

10
OVERCOMING TENSION

According to Dr. William C. Menninger, "Few people, if any, in the modern world escape psychological stress and strain of major proportions." Most jogging enthusiasts promise that if you are tense the best remedy is to put on your running gear and work off your emotional distress. This may be true for minor mental strain, but is no cure-all for larger problems.

Consider for example, how chronic resentment can produce stress. I recall Mrs. S, a housewife who had steadily mounting blood pressure. Her systolic reading remained around 200 in spite of the use of newer drugs to control it. Like the central character in a detective story, she remained a mysterious person. Improvement did not come until she admitted at last that she lived in daily tension. She hated a sister who had made a better marriage than herself. Not until she had a few talks with her sister and achieved an understanding with her did her blood pressure fall to near normal. "I could feel my tension peel off, layer by layer, after I confessed being sick with resentment."

Mr. M was executive vice-president who twice almost died in heart attacks. He also was a hater. Passed over for the presidency in his firm, he had simmered and boiled whenever he thought about, or came in contact with, the innocent colleague who had been given the top prize. Like Mrs. S, his improvement came about after he confessed to the new president his consuming hatred. At present he remains the chief's trusted associate and friend and says, "I wouldn't take the pressure of being president if it was handed to me on a platter." Mr. M. is no longer a "successful failure."

Mrs. T couldn't bear to look at her old refrigerator, her old living room furniture, or her three-year-old car because her neighbor was so much better off than she was. She nagged her husband so much that he lost confidence in his ability to work. Their sexual compatability was also threatened. The home was filled with hostility, bickering, and nervous children, but no amount of philosophizing or practical advice helped her. Under constant tension, she suffered a heart attack and died one year later at 48 while filing for divorce.

It's apparent that each of us must be able to adjust—physically and emotionally—to the environment into which life thrusts us. We must build our individual barriers against engulfing tensions. The solution depends upon us rather than upon others. If jogging relieves your tensions, I recommend it—if you are physically fit. However, what I have been trying to tell you here is that there are other ways to relieve tension: by trying to remove the tension at its source, at its cause. Remember that it isn't the load that brings us down; it's the way we carry it.

Here are some stressful conditions that may arise during a lifetime. How you carry such loads may be the difference between continued good health and a heart attack:

- Marriage (arguments with a spouse)
- Divorce
- Death of a close family member
- Death of a spouse
- Death of a close friend
- Personal illness or injury
- Severe illness in a family member
- Being fired from work
- Changing job
- Change in financial status
- Sexual difficulties

It's evident that your susceptibility to a heart attack may be influenced by your position in the social environment, by changes in that environment, and by personal changes that influence your life.

THE BIG T

I call tension the "Big T." Even though you seem to be all right now, excessive tension will weaken your coronary arteries. Mental stress is the enemy. Call it stress or tension, it will take it out of you somewhere—ulcer, hypertension, diabetes, overactive thyroid, ulcerative colitis, and so on. The heart attack is the most dangerous of all. You know how your heart races and pounds during sudden fear. Then consider what happens to the coronary arteries when they are subjected to tension for hours, days, and weeks. Excessive adrenalin production is part of the problem of atherosclerosis.

Tension has a cumulative effect. After years of unnatural stress, arteries weaken. Learning how to live a relaxed way is, in my opinion, the most essential antidote to the threat of potential heart attack. Learning how to unstress yourself may take time but it is worth the effort.

I think there is too much emphasis on the heart, or the pump, and not enough on the arteries, the pipes. If it is true, as exerters believe, that exercise strengthens the heart and prolongs life, how beneficial is exercise for the arteries?

What possible good can overexertion produce on the artery walls? Jogging may temporarily reduce the cholesterol level in the blood but can it remove existing cholesterol and calcium deposits? Can jogging transform stiff arteries into supple ones? What is the good of a strong heart when the pipes it feeds with blood are occluded and the circulation impeded? Jogging may improve collateral circulation, but so may the aging process.

We should consider total fitness, which is not a matter of the strength of the heart muscle itself or of the size of the biceps or leg muscles. Overexercise is wasted energy because it performs a lopsided service, if it saves the heart, which is questionable and certainly unproved, it does nothing for the arteries except invite possible complications that may endanger the entire organism.

There is a need, therefore, to reconsider the relative values of exertion and relaxation to keep arteries supple. This is more important than muscle suppleness. Arteries thrive on minimal tension, on absence of abnormal amounts of adrenaline in the blood stream. For fitness, rather than attempt to strengthen an already normal heart, I would prefer to look for ways to save the arteries from early deterioration. This, as I will show later, you can accomplish by sitting in a rocker and refusing to jog or otherwise tax your muscles.

You slowly kill yourself if you think you can carry any load so long as you exercise to keep fit if you run your life by any of these common misconceptions:

If you disregard bad heredity.

If you spell tension with a small "t."

If you try to squeeze twenty-eight hours into twenty-four.

If you allow chronic resentment to induce daily tension.

If you continue in a job you hate.

If you are unduly fond of pressure.

If you expose your middle-aged arteries to excessive stress.

If you do not guard against social stresses.

If you do not believe that stress contributes to heart attacks.

Here is part of an editorial that appeared in the *Journal of Human Stress* (June 1975): "It is generally acknowledged that stress is a contributory factor to illness and death, and that it is increasingly important for physicians and researchers to be aware of the roles it plays in our living and dying."

Both husband and wife should realize the potential dangers of a tension-filled home in causing heart attacks. Working like two blades of a pair of scissors, neither spouse should ask which contributes more to a tension-free home. Only such a shared approach will reduce the danger of a heart attack in either husband or wife. Disabuse yourself, moreover, of the belief that only husbands suffer heart attacks.

Wives and husbands know what tension is. They know what makes the other nervous and tense. If you want to keep him or her around longer, you must develop individual ways to keep your spouse relaxed and happy. I realize this isn't easy. Husbands can't expect wives to be saintly, to endure servitude. It takes two to make tension—or to provide for the lack of it.

For example, consider Mrs. A:

What I am most afraid of is that my husband may come down with a heart attack. If not that, with a stroke. Probably you have already guessed what his trouble is. It's tension. He's always wound up like a spring, stretched out like a rubber band.

He claims I'm borrowing trouble. "I'm only 43," he says. "I keep my weight down and don't drink more than a jigger of bourbon a day. I don't smoke. I jog at least three miles every day. Why keep worrying I'll get a heart attack?"

What worries me is that he hasn't had a physical checkup in years. How does he know his heart is strong enough to take the jogging? But he laughs at that. Also when I tell him he doesn't relax enough. He works at least twelve hours a day in the office. He often takes his work home at night.

He doesn't even sit down to watch TV with the family. He gets upset and gets into rages over little things. I forgive him because I know he's exhausted. With it all, he insists on jogging when he's so tired. Says it's good for him, although he doesn't seem to enjoy it. Does it only because he says "it's good for me." Good for what? How can his heart stand it?

Mrs. A promised to bring her husband in—drag him in—for an examination. Although I intended to pin a few gold stars on him for not smoking, overdrinking, overeating, and all that, I told Mrs. A that he would get quite a lecture for jogging at his age without having had a stress test.

Many women ask me how to reduce their husbands' tensions. They want them to wean themselves away from work pressures and tranquilizers. There is no one remedy that will work for all. Jogging will do it for some, but it becomes the responsibility of the patient himself to find a way. Let me tell you about a unique method I heard about while on my way to a medical convention in Atlantic City.

I purchased my ticket at the bus terminal in New York City, and while waiting for the bus to load, I started small talk with a middle-aged man who seemed as excited about the bus trip as a small boy on his first outing. "I look forward to this once every month," he said.

> I leave my car and family home, and I buy a round trip ticket to some place on the Jersey shore. Today it's Atlantic City. I'll be home tonight.
> I'm completely relaxed from the moment I buy my ticket. I let the bus driver do the worrying for me. And when I arrive at the resort I'll walk up and down that boardwalk and look out at the ocean and take deep breaths of the clean, pure air. When I come home, I feel like a new man.
> I'm better for myself and for my family. A person has to be by himself every once in a while. The entire trip costs me less than a bottle or two of tranquilizers used to stand me. I've talked my wife into doing the same, and she takes a trip with one of her girl friends while I stay home to mind the kids.

Each one of us must find our own formula to prevent excessive stress. There are many antidotes at hand. I recall a neighbor, a busy executive, who found complete relief from tension by taking in a movie alone during a prolonged lunch hour every week or two. A homemaker I knew would get a similar effect by shutting herself off for an hour or two and listening to hi-fi.

A certain amount of stress is essential for survival, but when too much daily stress adds up to unremitting tension, it's more likely that your coronary arteries will rebel. Examine your lifestyle. Step out of your skin to look at yourself impartially. Be willing to make changes, to jog or not to jog, to shift from high gear to low. And often to neutral—just idling.

William Glaser in his book *Positive Addiction* (New York: 1976, Harper and Row) wrote,

> Most of us spend our lives in a series of compromises between doing what we believe in and doing what will please those who are important to us. Happiness depends a great deal on gaining enough strength to live with a minimum of these compromises.

Writing in the *Miami Herald* (December 5, 1978), Richard M.

Restak of the Washington Post Service calls exercise "The opiate of the people":

> We have no indisputable evidence, contrary to what you've been hearing and reading, that exercise will make you healthier, live longer, and reap psychological benefits that will transform your life into a happy pattern of existence. It's possible that rigorous exercise may be good for your neighbor, yet be "poison" for you. Exercise enthusiasts who make extravagant claims rarely issue warnings of potential disaster—whether major or minor.

HOW TO RELIEVE TENSION

The reason I call tension the Big T is because it can throw the proverbial wrench into your body's machinery. Tension is the cause—or at least the contributing cause—of many diseases. Of all the supposed causes of heart attacks, I rate tension number one—ahead of such threatening enemies as high blood cholesterol, high triglycerides, overweight, hypertension, and lack of exercise. The relaxed fat man has less chance of having a heart attack than the one in "good physical shape," who believes that jogging is the antidote for tension-filled days.

My neighbor's friend, visiting from out of town, said that her husband, 38, considers himself to be a middle-aged athlete. He jogs three times a week and does pushups every morning and night. But she doesn't think he's in good condition. According to his doctor, his blood pressure is beginning to climb, and he has some slight changes in his electrocardiogram. The doctor has advised him to slow down, give up jogging for a while, but he insists on having his workouts.

He rushes to work, overworks at the office, and rushes home to change into his shorts and sneakers. He is tense and always reaching for a cigarette and a highball.

"In spite of what the doctor and I tell him," the visitor explained, "he considers himself a perfect physical specimen because of jogging. He won't slow down. I'm really worried. Is there anything I can tell this lovable young fool so I can have him around quite a few more years?"

I told her that excessive smoking and drinking are only surface manifestations of abnormal tension. He seems to be hurrying all the time, trying to catch up. He's probably the type who dashes to the airport just in time to run to the plane. There are several ways to fight off tension, and my advice to the woman for her husband went something like this:

One simple, beneficial tip is to set the clock a half hour to one hour earlier in the morning. This will give him time for a leisurely breakfast. He won't have to rush to the office. When he has an appointment, have him start early so he won't have to stew while stranded in traffic and send his pressure higher.

Gradually, this will improve his braking system and keep him from working and playing in high gear. Constantly fighting against the clock is a daily piling up of dangerous tension.

There are scores of other ways to live at a slower pace, but have him try this first. You'll be surprised, as he will, how much more pleasant and healthful it is when you can twiddle your thumbs waiting for a plane, instead of straining your arteries trying to catch it before the doors close.

As for his jogging against doctor's orders, perhaps reading this book will help him make the decision to keep fit by using the alternate methods I describe in this book.

Whoever you are, wherever you are, and whatever you do, it is undeniable that you live in tension. A minimal amount of it is essential for survival. Your muscles are tense even when they rest; they have to be taut enough to prevent your skeleton from dangling.

The secret is in learning how to control excess tension, so it will not produce bodily harm. Admittedly, hypertension, high cholesterol, smoking, diabetes, and obesity are all important precursors of a heart attack. So is poor heredity. What I have been saying is that too much tension affects all these factors.

If you are tense day after day, the chances are that it will send your blood pressure up. The more tense you are, the more you will smoke. If you are abnormally tense, it's likely that you will require more insulin to control your diabetes. Tense? You'll eat more and get fat, possibly raising your blood lipids (cholesterol and triglycerides).

I recall many patients whose blood pressure, obesity, and bad smoking habits greatly improved when they learned how to live in less tension. One man quickly shucked his cigarette habit. Another cut down on his snacking when he gave up an unhappy job and took one that gave him pleasure.

You need to learn how to reduce abnormal tension. Your family doctor may help; so may a psychologist or a psychotherapist. So may you, yourself, by learning relaxation programs such as Transcendental Meditation (TM), progressive relaxation, and other methods.

Once you have learned how to reduce abnormal tension, you will reduce your heart rate, lower your blood pressure, and condition yourself how to meet the various stresses found in your home, job, and social life.

First, be aware of what tension is. Many who live in tension do not realize they are driving their machines unmercifully. (Among those are tense persons who jog, excessively, believing that this activity covers all ills like a blanket.) Instead, they are asking for trouble— physical, emotional or psychological. It is important to take time out to evaluate your way of life, whatever your age. Without being aware that tension may be your enemy, you will have little hope to overcome it in time to prevent serious damage.

A wife complained to me about her husband's bad temper. She explained that he flares up like an explosion when least expected. He has high blood pressure, had an exceptionally serious heart attack, and is now taking up jogging to "soothe his nerves." When he suddenly erupts he gets red in the face, bangs on the table and walls, and even throws things. Once he pitched a bookend through the TV set. What concerns her most is the possibility that he may bring on another heart attack.

A temper tantrum is like the swish of a dragon's tail—it is terrible to behold, and it leaves many innocent, wounded people in its wake. The sudden release of adrenalin flooding the arteries of the brain and heart surely isn't doing the weakened arteries of the tension-filled patient any good.

Vacations often help people with temper problems. However, unless taken sensibly, even vacations can be harmful. Dr. Jean Mayer, president of Tuft's University, wrote this in Family Health (August 1977):

> If, on the other hand, frenzied activity is your thing, take the If-this-is-Tuesday-it-must-be-Belgium approach to your vacation. Don't listen to naysayers like me who claim that too much exercise is as bad—both physically and psychologically—as too little exercise. Try to cram everything you can into a few short weeks.

TIPS ON HOW TO ENJOY A VACATION

A wife wrote complaining that it was difficult to convince her husband to take vacations:

> He is one of those hard workers who says he loves his job so much he doesn't require vacations. But after the furious pace during the year he begins to look exhausted. I tell him he has a duty to himself and us to relax before he comes down with a coronary attack.
>
> So he inevitably gives in. But there's so much effort expended by all of us before, during, and after vacation, I sometimes wonder if it wouldn't be better to stay home.
>
> I've often read that you consider too much tension an enemy. Under the circumstances, don't you think I'm right in having him take a vacation every year?

The body is a machine, and one should take time for a yearly overhaul. Even machines need periods of rest, and man needs them even more. He has few, if any, replaceable parts. There are mental, emotional, and physical components that require rejuvenation. The following suggestions will help to make your yearly problems more bearable:

1. To take a vacation really means to "vacate"—to get away, to get out of oneself. It should, if possible, be a complete change from the usual routine. For example, I often tell people to leave their books at home if they're insatiable readers. If they play golf every day when at home, I suggest they take books instead of golf sticks. Most golfers and readers would abhor such advice, but those who have tried it say it works.

2. Whether you should take vacations together as a family depends on many personal factors. Some wives and husbands find that separate vacations for a week or so make the partnership so much more rewarding when they come back together.

3. Be willing to make compromises. If your wife did not enjoy the seashore last year, agree to try the mountains this year. If your husband gets seasick on a cruise, don't try to convince him to take another against his will.

4. Someone who has been physically active during the year is entitled to a lazy vacation. Snoozing in a hammock or on the grass shouldn't make such a person feel self-conscious.

5. Someone who has been physically inactive should be discouraged from becoming a middle-aged athlete for a few weeks a year. Too strenuous activity may bring on an accident or serious illness. Vacations are important, but how you take them may be even more important.

Unplanned vacations often turn into periods of unnecessary stress rather than islands of relaxation. Here are some additional tips on how to enjoy vacations:

• Plan your vacations some time ahead. I've known people who came home tired from a month's vacation because they were bored. Being workaholics, they pined for work after only a few days of absence. Such persons should take four one-week vacations a year rather than swallow it all in one large bite. For others, several three-day weekends are more enjoyable than any other kind of vacation.

• If you wear dentures or glasses, be sure to take along an extra pair.

• Some friends of mine recently returned from a trip that was marred by the excess baggage and inappropriate, unnecessary clothes they found themselves lugging around.

• A common cause of upsets during vacations is the tendency to overeat and overdrink while away. Try to avoid these excesses and you will spend less time taking pills for nausea and diarrhea.

• Ladies should be conscious of taking along comfortable walking shoes.

• Arrange your schedule so that you don't get right back to work the day you return. Leave a day or two for sorting out your mail and getting your bearings.

If you follow these suggestions and decompress gradually, there is less likelihood that you will complain, one day after you return, "I don't feel as if I've been away. I'm as tense as I was before I went on vacation."

Too many vacationers return conscience stricken because they weren't sufficiently active while away. You will err less, if you have been relaxing most of the time rather than being overactive.

11

KEEP FIT BY CONTROLLING HABITS

"I'm stale. I guess I need some exercise." Have you ever said that? It's as common as banal remarks about the weather.

I am asking you to resolve instead to make relaxation, rather than exercise, the hub of your conditioning program. Beware of overexertion when your waistline bulges and your hairline recedes. Modern life saps energy reserves, and although your arteries are elastic, when they age, they will stretch just so far. Don't overstretch. Remember, too, that the middle-aged heart isn't as normal as a youngster's, even though the electrocardiograms seem similar.

Don't be deluded into thinking that if you don't exercise daily you will surely deteriorate prematurely. Athletic fitness and good health are not synonymous. Don't turn to jogging as a cure-all. Instead, first take inventory of the possible reasons for that stale feeling. What else in your life-style or physical condition may be the answer to your problem of being unfit rather than fit? Do you smoke? Do you drink too much? Do you have unsuspected diabetes or hypertension? Do you know how to relax?

I'll help you answer these questions, and you will come to look upon jogging as an aberration of the twentieth century. History is replete with examples of similar irrational and unexplainable activities.

ALCOHOL AND HEART DISEASE

An important element in your examination of your physical condition is to determine whether you're a social drinker or an alcoholic. Perhaps controlling your alcohol intake is all you need to be in fine shape.

There have been many definitions of alcoholism. I think a person is an alcoholic if he (or she) takes abnormal amounts of alcohol in any form daily and if this interferes with the fulfillment of business, social, or family responsibilities. Some, of course, are weekend alcoholics.

The dividing line between the chronic alcoholic and the social drinker is quite thin. I recall many business and professional workers who prided themselves on holding their liquor. If you accused them of being addicted, they were enraged. Yet, they were alcoholics: three martinis at lunch; two bottles of beer with the main course; two or three swigs in the afternoon from a bottle stashed away in the office desk; a few highballs at dinner; two or three beers at night while watching TV; and being sure to go overboard at a cocktail or dinner party. What a haul!

These so-called social drinkers were alcoholics and didn't suspect it. If they did, they didn't admit it. After soaking up alcohol daily, their arteries were carrying heavy loads of it; they were transporting blood overloaded with fats. Liver cells were being insulted daily; they were gathering and reserving resentment for the day when they would rise up in concerted revolt as cirrhosis of the liver.

The theory that alcohol may also be bad for the heart is something relatively new. In treating angina patients, Joan Orlando, M.D., and her associates noted that an "abnormally rapid increase in heart rate and in systolic blood pressure with exercise also occurred after ingestion of ethanol (alcohol). This situation is very similar to that observed after the ingestion of a meal." They also noted that angina after exercise came on earlier after five ounces of ethanol than after taking two ounces. They believe that the anesthetic effect of five ounces of ethanol may mask earlier recognition of anginal pain. (Joggers, please note!)

Another investigator seems to agree. In a communication on alcohol and heart disease addressed to physicians, Lawrence D. Horwitz, M.D., of the University of Texas Health Science Center at San Antonio, writes, "Unfortunately, many physicians are unaware that alcohol may have detrimental effects on the heart. This is not surprising since for centuries there has been a widespread misconception, promulgated in textbooks of medicine, that alcohol is a cardiac stimulant.' " Horwitz says there is strong evidence that alcohol is a heart depressant. He claims that those with severe heart damage and chronic heart failure should probably not drink at all. Other heart patients should be limited to a maximum daily of one shot of one and one-half ounces of whiskey, one twelve-ounce can of beer, or one six-ounce glass of wine. Furthermore, patients with coronary disease should be warned that for two hours after drinking, they should refrain from activity that could induce angina.

Other researchers have found definite evidence that large amounts of alcohol taken daily produced significant rises in blood cholesterol and triglycerides. Although all these are potential enemies of coronary circulation, doctors still differ in the evaluation of the risks of alcohol. I believe that if a patient with coronary disease has lasted into his late sixties or early seventies, this is proof enough that his habit of taking an ounce or two of whiskey has been helpful rather than harmful. I do not deny him this small, apparently harmless comfort in his old age.

However, if you are in your forties or fifties, you had better assume that a daily intake of three or four cans of beer, a half bottle of wine, or two or three shots of hard liquor would not be helpful to your heart. You also risk liver damage. In people with severe heart disease, even one or two cocktails may decrease heart performance. According to one theory, alcohol interferes with magnesium storage in the heart muscle. This may cause heart failure by producing a condition called cardiomyopathy. Such patients should abstain entirely from liquor, eat a nutritious diet, avoid salt, and take diuretics if necessary. Cigarettes and coffee are also taboo.

The angina patient considering heart surgery should not drink for a few weeks before the operation. This will help spare the liver, which will have the job of detoxifing the elements used during anesthesia.

As I've said, doctors still differ about the effects of alcohol on the heart and arteries. Some even say that heavy drinkers are less likely to develop atherosclerosis. No clinical studies support unequivocally either theory, however.

All the experiments and resulting differences of opinion have at least removed any complacency that alcohol is invariably good for heart patients and others. At least we are now alerted that alcohol may be harmful rather than helpful for both the sick and the well. Moderation is still the byword.

What I have been saying is especially important for many joggers who are in the habit of taking liquor before or after the run. It's evident that if they have unrecognized coronary disease, the alcohol may bring on an attack of angina or worse.

Nonjoggers should make an honest estimate of their status: social drinker or alcoholic? In either case, cutting down or "out" will surely contribute to better health and fitness without the need to jog or do calisthenics.

A few weeks ago I met a colleague at a cocktail party. At 60 he prided himself on being fit. A recent convert to jogging, he had a tendency to overload on occasion. That evening he really put away those martinis until he was like a drunken sailor walking deck in a hurricane. His wife was not with him, and I insisted on driving him home or calling a cab for him. He stubbornly refused, saying he would wait a few minutes and he would be all right. I lost sight of him for a few minutes and did not see him leave. Within the hour we received word that he had struck a guard-rail at high speed and was killed. I keep wondering why I wasn't more insistent in driving him home. I know alcohol can be a killer. I have a sense of guilt, but at least I tried.

An alcoholic can be stubborn. You have seen many and so have I. A cocktail party is not the only potentially dangerous watering hole. Liquor drunk at a dinner party, at an ordinary business luncheon, or in solitude also can dull the driving reflexes, or practically obliterate them. Alcohol was the cause of at least 25,000 traffic fatalities in 1978. Such figures include, of course, not just chronic alcoholics, but also moderate drinkers who become menaces to themselves and others after just one or two drinks.

Here are some safety rules. The best tip is not to drink at all immediately before driving. If you take an ounce of hard liquor, wait at least one hour for the body to use it up. Two highballs? Wait about two hours before driving.

A general rule is to give the body at least an hour to totally absorb the effects of one one-ounce drink. If you have three highballs by 9:00 P.M. (all within a short time and on an empty stomach) driving home at midnight will be safer than taking off at 10:00 P.M. Absorption of alcohol into the blood stream is faster on an empty stomach. Taking food will prevent the alcohol from making a sudden assault on the brain with the consequent loss of proper control of one's senses.

The best advice I can give is to rely on a sober friend or taxi driver for transportation home if you are intoxicated. As the sad case of my colleague proved, driving while drunk is like driving with a loaded gun at your head. One never knows when it will go off.

When I see young women jogging to keep fit, I wonder how many in the child-bearing age realize that the few highballs they take at night are serious threats to their own fitness and to that of an unborn child. A patient of mine expressed concern about a sister with an alcohol problem. A stickler for physical fitness and a determined jogger, the sister was a heavy drinker. She was also thinking of getting married, at 32, because saw this as her "last chance to have a child." She promised to cut down on her drinking after she got married. But my patient wondered if it wasn't true that alcohol might harm the baby.

I suggested that for the sake of herself, her husband-to-be, and her unborn baby, the sister should not get married until she informed her boyfriend of the problem and asked help from her doctor and Alcoholics Anonymous. To continue to drink would invite pregnancy complications.

A bulletin by the Department of Health, Education and Welfare warns about the potential dangers of drinking during pregnancy. The bulletin says that excessive use of alcohol during pregnancy may produce what's called the fetal alcohol syndrome, which consists of a variety of malformations in the limbs, heart, face, head, and elsewhere. Alcohol also increases the incidence of stillbirths and spontaneous abortions. Pregnant women should especially refrain from binge drinking. In a recent study, 32 percent of the infants born to heavy drinkers had congenital abnormalities compared to nine percent in those who did not drink and 14 percent in moderate drinkers. There is a clear risk when the pregnant woman ingests the equivalent of three ounces of absolute alcohol, or about six drinks per day. The risk for lesser amounts is uncertain, but caution is advised.

Physicians should discuss drinking habits with women in the child-bearing age. To play safe, pregnant women should not exceed two drinks in a single day, even if they normally drink alcoholic beverages only once a week, month, or year. The alcohol problem is greater than many women realize, especially during pregnancy.

If the heart patient in your family has become an alcoholic—or if the alcoholic has become a heart patient—here are some practical suggestions on how to manage the problem. Some of these important don'ts are also subscribed to by the Al-Anon Group, which is so helpful in advising family members of alcoholics being treated by Alcoholics Anonymous.

First, you must be convinced that the alcoholic is sick and not sinful. Learning what not to do is an important part of the program: Don't treat the alcoholic like a naughty child; you wouldn't if he were suffering from some other disease. Don't check up to see how much the alcoholic is drinking. Don't search for hidden liquor. Don't pour liquor away. The alcoholic always finds ways to get more. Don't refer to the drinking problem in any way until the alcoholic indicates a desire to talk about it. Never talk about it while the alcoholic is under the influence of alcohol. Don't preach, reproach, scold, or enter into quarrels.

If you can bring yourself to avoid these things, you'll be well on the way to a more comfortable frame of mind. All these don'ts have good sound reasons that grew out of many people's experience.

The alcoholic suffers from feelings of guilt beyond anything the nonalcoholic can imagine. Reminding him of failures and social errors or of his neglect of family and friends is all wasted effort. It only makes the situation worse. The suffering alcoholic has bitterly blamed himself a thousand times over, and your reminders are unbearably painful. Moreover, guard against a holier than thou attitude that reflects hostility, skepticism, or contempt.

All you can do is hope that some day the alcoholic will ask for help. Let the repentant sufferer do the talking. To the desperate question "What shall I do?" simply say you know things that can be done. If asked for suggestions, you can then be specific, mentioning AA or whatever other source of help you may have found available.

SMOKING

"Smokers die more frequently within the first fifteen minutes of a heart attack than do non-smokers," said Dr. David M. Spain, director of medical affairs at Brookdale Hospital Center, Brooklyn, speaking at the Nineteenth Annual Scientific Session of the American College of Cardiology. His study showed that among 189 men who died suddenly from heart disease, 15 out of every 16 were heavy cigarette smokers, and most were under the age of 50. The smokers were ten to twelve years younger than the nonsmokers. Smokers also survived a shorter time after the onset of the attack, and they died too soon for revival techniques to help or be initiated. Spain found that there appears to be a close association between cigarette smoking and sudden death.

I have talked to joggers who say that quitting tobacco and other bad habits is one of the favorable by-products of this exercise.

Nevertheless, many joggers still smoke. Rex Reed recently interviewed Burt Lancaster: "Lighting an unfiltered Camel, Lancaster, still glistening with perspiration from having jogged five miles to this interview, sets up the first of many paradoxes studding both his professional and personal life. 'I know,' he said, 'I live in a land full of health nuts and still I smoke. I run every day to offset the effect.' "

Unfortunately, so do thousands of other joggers, who believe that jogging neutralizes and acts as an antidote for such heart threats as smoking, overeating, overdrinking. If you hope to be fit and healthy, quit smoking. This includes pipes and cigars as well as cigarettes. At an International Conference on Lung Diseases, Dr. Allan L. Goldman said that inhaling cigar smoke may be more harmful than inhaling cigarette smoke. In spite of what you hear to the contrary, most patients who switch from cigarettes to cigars continue to inhale. Many innocent cigar smokers have come in confessing to smoking a dozen cigars a day and adding, "But, as you know, doctor we cigar smokers don't inhale, so we know they can't hurt you."

How is tobacco a threat to your health? By now most know the answer: potential coronary heart disease, serious involvement of the leg arteries, emphysema, chronic bronchitis, lung cancer, and other variations of human suffering.

Are you willing to quit? There are almost as many ways of giving up the weed as there are smokers. According to one Californian, all you need do is eliminate one cigarette a day until you are down to zero. That is "cure day." It's really a painless countdown: 20, 19, 18, 17. . . . Try it. Many temperaments will accept gradual cutdown, but will not agree to sudden application of the brakes and the resultant skids and squeals.

But others prefer the short, full stop. For example, consider President Dwight D. Eisenhower's methods of quitting. He told me about it when I was alone with him for about a half hour in Gettysburg on November 27, 1967.

He had been a four-packs-a-day smoker. His doctors asked him to quit while he was in Augusta, Georgia, recuperating from an attack of ileitis after the war. Determined to overcome the habit, he devised a carefully planned battle campaign to subjugate nicotine. His plan included constant and unflinching exposure of himself to attack.

I purposely surrounded myself with packs of cigarettes. I scattered them about the house. On the TV set, at my bedside, on tables, books, and chairs. At every turning my will was challenged by tantalizing packs of cigarettes. But I refused to weaken. I considered it a fight, a battle. When guests came I would personally offer them cigarettes. I would light matches or present them with a ligher before they could reach their own. I won the battle. I haven't smoked since.

Whichever method you choose, there are three prerequisites for success: proper motivation, willpower, and a method you have chosen for yourself.

There is medical disagreement about whether obesity or smoking is more harmful, but the weight of opinion, I believe, is on the side which believes that there is greater danger when you smoke. According to one statistician, you would have to gain 120 pounds to equal the potential danger involved in smoking two packs a day. What I can state unequivocally is that neither obesity or tobacco is good for you.

When you smoke, think of what you inhale—nicotine and the other toxic chemicals that raise blood pressure, produce changes in blood and lungs, and cause ECG changes that indicate trouble in the coronary arteries. Think of the carbon monoxide that accumulates in the blood. This robs the coronary arteries of needed oxygen, since hemaglobin in the blood has at least 200 times greater affinity for carbon monoxide than for combining with oxygen. You can understand why smokers are more prone to suffer from angina pectoris.

According to Dr. Spain, "Among the environmental factors thought to be associated with the course of an acute episode of ischemia (heart attack) are cigarette smoking and physical activity." In the autopsy reports of the 189 men who died suddenly and unexpectedly and whom Spain studied, it was found that the men were from varied walks of life and ranged from sedentary to fairly active individuals. None were under a doctor's care for a heart condition!

For years women believed that they were immune from coronary attacks. Studies have shown, however, that cigarette smoking has also caused a rise in fatal heart attacks in women. In the 1950s there were twelve sudden deaths in men from coronary heart disease for each one in women. By the late 1960s the ratio had dropped to 4 to one. This shift has been associated with an increase in heavy smoking among women; heavy smoking may cut a woman's life span as much as nineteen years. It's evident, then, that for men and women, another lazy way to keep fit without jogging is to have the determination and willpower to quit smoking.

Wearing a pin-striped suit and a deep blue tie, the nattily dressed 43-year-old executive drew on his cigarette and said, "Of course I've heard all about the potential dangers of lung cancer from cigarettes. But what I'm especially interested in is the chance of getting emphysema.

"I've smoked since I was 15. My doctor says I already have a bad case of chronic bronchitis. He says it isn't emphysema yet, but if I keep on smoking I might die. Frankly, I'm beginning to lose my cool. He frightened me. Is tobacco really such a menace? I smoke only one and a half packs a day."

I looked at him and said that there is little doubt in the minds of most doctors that smoking cigarettes year after year is like pouring drops of gasoline on a flame. Smoke keeps on irritating the bronchial tubes and the lung surfaces until inflammatory changes take place. Even the cilia that line the tubes become ineffective. Mucus collects in the lungs and produces coughing and expectoration.

Emphysema, in which there is actual destruction of the air sacs of the lungs, is a common complication of bronchitis, and it is often brought on by excessive smoking. After a while the patient gets short of breath. Soon he can't walk a block or two without gasping for air. Worse still, he fights for air even when he is at rest in a chair or in bed. Later, his heart weakens, and it's right side fails.

The businessman looked at me quizically and asked for a tray so he could stub out the remainder of his cigarette. He stuck his hand in a coat pocket, withdrew a pack of cigarettes, and with careful aim tossed it over the rim of a wastebasket. He said, "Sometimes it takes a damn good scare to make a fool into a sensible human being."

Do you smoke? Does your husband smoke? Many a parent who smokes is the real reason why some youngsters begin to take up cigarette smoking early. "Do as I say, not as I do," you may tell them, but that does little good. However, if you say you'll quit and do, a child will often take up your lead and quit smoking, too—or, better still, not begin.

In my experience it's almost a waste of breath to try to scare a youngster into quitting or not starting. Paint all the dreadful pictures of suffering due to angina, emphysema, and lung cancer, and the youngster thinks, "Not everyone gets these complications. Chances are I won't either."

Why look so far into the future? Now is what concerns the young. Let's tell them that smoking interferes with their jogging. Let's say that it interferes with their real enjoyment of food. Let's tell them that smoking may cut down their wind if they play tennis or engage in other sports. Let's say that a brain starved for oxygen (displaced by carbon monoxide in cigarette smoke) may not adequately prepare for tomorrow's exam. Let's tell them that if they're looking for a job, smoking may lessen their chances if their employer-to-be happens to be a nonsmoker.

I wish we could truthfully tell a youngster, "Smoking interferes with your sex appeal. Every time a girl or boy sees you light up, it turns them off." What might help most would be disallowing TV and movie characters to smoke on screen. Impressionable youngsters tend to be copycats as they watch their heroes and heroines nonchalantly reach for cigarettes, pipes, or cigars.

Whatever the method, if it works, we should try it. It's easier not to start smoking than to stop.

Sometimes, enumerating some of the symptoms that smoking can cause will alert the young to the dangers of smoking. According to one homemaker who quit smoking, some of the bad effects smokers can expect are shortness of breath, tightness in chest area, headaches, coughing, weak knees, poor circulation, occasional numbness in fingers and toes, itching and burning eyes, quick temper, nervousness, quick to tire, accelerated pulse, poor gums and loose teeth, peeling and splitting of nails, crow's feet lines around eyes from squinting through smoke, stale odor, and many, many more undesirable consequences.

I recall one 18-year-old, two-pack-a-day smoker who quit cold turkey after the family doctor told him that it was the tobacco responsible for his "face full of pimples."

"It worked like the proverbial charm," my colleague said. "I'm glad the kid didn't realize I was only joking. As far as I know, there's no evidence that smoking causes acne."

I act as referee for two physician friends of mine who sheepishly admit to bad habits. Both have taken up jogging, but knowing I'm not in favor of it, they never bring this exercise into the discussion. One overeats, the other oversmokes. They believe that jogging will lessen their desire to eat and smoke. At times their differences of opinion gets so hot I have to separate them.

One of the doctors looks up statistics which apparently prove that smoking's worse for one than obesity. The other brings in some medical clippings which prove that obesity is worse than smoking.

As a referee, all I can do is keep them apart, but frankly, I'm as much in the dark as they are. I think that many doctors are confused about the relative dangers of tobacco and obesity. After reading so many of the pros and cons, I believe that people who put away at least two packs a day for years are in greater danger than those who do not smoke and become obese.

We know, of course, that too much weight may lead to diabetes, hypertension, and heart disease. I say "may." These complications are serious but not inevitable. Nevertheless, I advise obese patients to lose and play safe.

I am less confident that the heavy smoker can escape serious complications. If not lung or throat cancer, he's at least likely to develop emphysema or severe chronic bronchitis. But the main danger in smoking, I believe, is the bad effect tobacco has on the blood vessels in the heart, brain, kidneys, and extremities. The smoker invites heart attack, stroke, or kidney failure later on.

Suppose you are thin and smoke? You rationalize, "Why quit? I'm sure I'll gain. Obesity is dangerous." That's only an excuse and rationalization. It's not inevitable that smokers who quit will gain weight.

But suppose you smoke and are fat? Then you'll have to meet the challenge of trying to overcome two bad habits at the same time. Call me joykiller now? Years from now you may call me joymaker.

I've been reading lately that government authorities are now considering a change in the labels of painkillers like aspirin. Instead of promising that the pills are good for arthritis, headache, and other ills, they will promise to temporarily help the pain. I wonder what they base their hopes on. The so-called success of the labels on cigarette packs?

I have often wondered just how many in a hundred smokers read the warning when they buy the new pack or when they reach for another cigarette. Two? Five? Any? Personally, I think it's a waste of energy. As you know, in spite of written warnings, as many or more cigarettes are now being consumed than ever before.

Instead, as I've suggested, why not get after TV sponsors and TV stations to actually ban the use of cigarettes not only in advertisements but by characters appearing before the camera? This should include everyone from actors in soap opera skits to politicians. I wonder how many of our cabinet members who appear on TV interview shows could survive the half hour without leaning on a pipe. Golda Meir smoked three packs a day, yet she rarely, if ever, smoked on TV for fear of influencing the young.

All this cigarette smoking before millions of youngsters undoubtedly acts as subliminal inducement to the smoking habit. This may be one reason why so many begin to smoke so early in life. They see these gorgeous gals and hands me leading men light up cigarettes, and the little monkey in them prompts them to go and do likewise.

THE COFFEE HABIT

A patient asked, "Don't you think that Americans drink too much coffee? At our office there are no lines in front of the water cooler. Instead, everyone seems to be standing around drinking cups of coffee. Isn't it harmful? I think of one friend, especially, who prides himself on being a jogger. Yet, he's developed a pot belly from drinking so much coffee—and eating the Danish that goes with it. How does he expect to be fit?"

I told her I'm a tea man myself. Take it in moderation. But I know enough to stay out of the way of the man or woman who simply must have that first cup of morning coffee "or die." Otherwise, they are not fit to live with. It brings out the worst in them. The sweetest Jekyl is a horrible Hyde until coffee produced its magic transformation. I also know that one or two coffee breaks during the day help promote working efficiency.

Undoubtedly, though, too much coffee is not good for the human machine. Many get away with it without apparent harm. Yet they may be unaware that six to ten cups of coffee daily may be the main reason why they are having heartburn, insomnia, palpitation, and jittery feelings—why they are on edge constantly. The caffeine gets to them.

One estimate is that Americans drink at least a billion cups of coffee yearly. I think that employers are also the losers. The coffee breaks they encourage for working efficiency have, in my opinion, turned into nothing more than excuses for letting up on the job.

I can understand the reasonableness of taking a coffee break in mid-afternoon to displace the accumulated tensions of the day, but seeing coffee, doughnuts, and Danish pastry dispensed on a cart as early as 10:00 A.M. while visiting a book publisher in Rockefeller Center in New York City, threw me off balance. Coffee so soon after breakfast and so close to lunch? It didn't make sense. I think the coffee break is overdone and contributes to much "unfitness." A break once in mid-afternoon is OK; otherwise it's a waste.

Since discovering how so many companies handle coffee breaks, I have become especially sensitive to the question of whether coffee breaks are overdone. Are they valid excuses to drop or not begin work? Are they really oases for refreshing body and spirit? Do they guarantee increased working efficiency?

My own feeling is that employers lose many millions of man and woman hours each year with the coffee break. Translate that into money lost, and you'd find it's large enough to nibble away at the national debt. Frankly, I can't understand why employers appear to accept this open-faced embezzlement so placidly.

But forgetting about employers, how about the employes? They get off less easily than they think, especially if they are fitness minded. Many an overweight problem—in spite of jogging—is due to several "coffee ands" during the day. Think too of the nervousness coffee breaks engender, instead of relaxation. The caffeine stimulates the pituitary gland, which in turn stimulates the pancreas, which puts out more insulin. Result: many chronic coffee-break addicts have a sharp fall in blood sugar. Unrecognized hypoglycemia (low blood sugar) causes nervousness, fatigue, and lack of efficiency.

The wife of a confirmed jogger had this to say about the coffee habit.

I tell my husband that he's addicted—not so much to jogging as to coffee. He used to be satisfied with two cups a day. But he has gradually increased his intake to as many as twelve or fifteen cups daily. I wouldn't mind except that he has been complaining of heartburn and heart skips lately. He is nervous and doesn't sleep well. I've kept coffee out of the house for a few days, but he would get so upset he'd get his coffee outside. So I had to bring it back into the house again.

I told her I doubted I'd be able to settle a family feud, but it was evident that her husband was addicted to coffee. Coffee drinkers develop an emotional and psychic dependence upon the drug. I believe it's important for her husband to take his coffee habit seriously—at least as seriously as his jogging. Taking as many as fifteen cups daily is enough to whip a person into trouble eventually.

Too much of a good thing—anything—is bad for the body. Too much exercise, too little exercise. Too much work, the boredom of too little work. Too much play, too little play. The body is resilient and accommodates itself, but extremes have their bad effects. So it is with eating and drinking. Overeating can be as bad as chronic starvation.

Coffee? A few cups a day—fine. But fifteen to twenty cups daily are much too many. Likewise, a daily drink of cola, fine. Ten bottles a day is too many. The caffeine in these drinks overstimulates the body.

Coffee has been in the news lately, not only because it's high priced. Some medical journal reports have stated that it produces heart attacks, that it raises blood pressure abnormally. Other doctors have disagreed. At present I feel that there is no specific proof that coffee, taken in moderate amounts, exerts deleterious effects upon the heart or arteries, but it can cause sharp drops in the level of blood sugar.

The following letter relates its effects on a patient who suffers from low blood sugar:

Dear Dr. Steincrohn,

This refers to the wife you wrote about making life miserable for husband and children because of her acute anxiety. How long will it be before doctors readily recognize the cause of this problem since those same symptoms—heart skips, nervousness, stomach trouble, and so on—occur in hundreds of thousands of individuals every year?

A pounding or skipping of the heartbeat, a feeling that one is about to faint or die, the side effects of anxiety or tiredness or depression, all these together are such a typical description of one common ailment, low blood sugar, that it amazes me this is not number one on the list of suspects rather than last or ignored completely.

How long will it be before doctors recognize that one of the primary culprits causing low blood sugar in certain people is caffeine? It's likely that wife you wrote about was drinking coffee or tea without anything else on her stomach when she had this acute sensation, causing her insulin-producing mechanism to be shocked into hyperactivity, causing her blood sugar level to fall.

I corrected a similar problem by eliminating coffee and caffeine. Please pass this along to that wife and perhaps to thousands of others who suffer needlessly.

I replied that some doctors do not believe there is such a syndrome as hypoglycemia, but I do. I also agree that caffeine often causes the blood sugar level to drop, but I do not agree that all cases of "acute anxiety" are due to unrecognized low blood sugar. Such nervous reactions may have no connection with the blood sugar level. Nevertheless, hypoglycemia should always be considered as a possibility.

There have been many instances in which blood sugar fell abruptly in joggers, in those who previously had normal blood sugar levels, and in those who were diabetic. What it all adds up to is that intake of excess caffeine is a detriment to fitness. As in everything else, moderation is the sensible answer.

But our main concern should be: how detrimental is coffee on the arteries themselves. *Archives of Internal Medicine* (October 1978) published a large-scale study conducted in Evans County, Georgia, an area that has been designated as "the Stroke Belt," and concluded that "neither coronary heart disease nor stroke death rates seem related to coffee-drinking habits."

It has been my experience that heavy coffee drinkers—those who consume more than six cups a day—are much more likely to smoke cigarettes. Or, perhaps, cigarette smokers are more likely to be heavy coffee drinkers. In either case, it's evident that cigarette smoking and other risk factors (hypertension, high cholesterol, and so on) bring on the heart attack rather than coffee consumption.

12

DO YOU KNOW HOW TO RELAX?

Tension is the common heritage of man, and woman, and child. Human beings are in a constant struggle to survive. The danger is that if we are not careful, we will live our lives on a treadmill of continuous exertions. Some people are able to bend with the wind of increased personal pressures, but too many break.

I've been calling undue tension the Big T for good reason. Next to poor heredity, tension is, in my opinion, the most potent factor in causing heart attacks. Hypertension, high cholesterol, diabetes, smoking, obesity—these are important causes, too. But stress that engulfs spirit and body and continues day after day is the enemy. There is a specific antidote for it: relaxation. Yet many do not take advantage of this remedy, and they suffer accordingly. I'll offer you a simple, effective way to relax. Call it a daily hibernation to regenerate yourself, to husband your energies. I'll not keep you in suspense any longer: it's the daily nap.

I have long been an advocate of the daily snooze, or snoozes, for those interested in uncomplicated methods of finding relaxation and fitness. Patients with hypertension, coronary disease, and ulcers have told me that daily snoozes helped them more than sedatives, tranquilizers, or tonics. It revitalized them by slowing them down in the face of tensions that had been driving them on and on. One patient said, "A nap is the most natural and satisfactory braking device that nature offers. It keeps you from running off the road."

The daily snooze helps neutralize the tensions that beset businessmen, housewives, and other workers. It is especially effective for the high-tension executive and the "house-driven" homemaker.

It requires practice to become a good snoozer. Some learn more easily than others, but once you master the art, you will never give it up. It freshens the spirit, gives the heart muscle a rest, and reinvigorates the body. It's like getting second wind.

When you nap for at least an hour a day you recharge the human body instead of killing it. Your blood pressure falls, your heart beats more slowly, you breathe easier, and your tensions are washed away for a while. For many, naps are lifesavers rather than killers.

A FEW MORE TIPS

Unquestionably, hobbies and frequent vacations are oases in the desert of tension and overactivity, but there are other ways to face up to daily stress. Too many of us get off on the wrong foot in the morning. We have overslept, or the alarm hasn't gone off, or we just hate to get out of bed at the appointed time. The rest of the day is spent in playing catch-up. Rushing through breakfast or missing breakfast entirely, boiling with resentment in traffic because you are late, bunching appointments, missing lunch, suffering through fatigue in mid-afternoon, and arriving home too tired to eat. There is an evident remedy. Set your clock one-half hour to one hour earlier, even though you lose some sleep. This head-start will start your day without tension and end it in relaxation. Try it for a week. See if it doesn't improve your way of life tremendously.

Immoderate use of the telephone adds layers of tension during the day. Talking too much on the phone upsets the balance of programs both at home and in the office. Try to find ways not to become enslaved by the ring of the telephone. Don't jump up at the first ring. Let it ring a few times. I've known one or two patients who sustained fractures of the leg in suddenly jumping up to run to the phone in a darkened room. Let your secretary collect your calls and set a time in the afternoon when you can return them in a relaxed frame of mind, rather than answering each call as it comes in and allowing it to interrupt whatever you happen to be doing at the time.

You may consider management of the clock and telephone as only minor matters in finding relaxation and absence of abnormal tension, but it is the little weights that soon add up to insufferable burdens too heavy to carry.

It's hard to believe that the rocking chair was invented right here in the United States—here in the land where we frown on siestas, where we rush through lunch standing up at a drugstore counter, where we look down in contempt upon the man relaxing in his hammock as we walk by with our bag of golf clubs.

Yes, it was about 1725 that some nameless American (who should have had a statue erected for him, sitting in his invention) had the imagination to see the need for his unique article of furniture. Forgetting about its origin for a while, it's interesting that there has been some revival of interest in the rocking chair.

I am proud to immodestly admit that I have been one of rocking chair's foremost boosters. As long ago as 1942, I wrote,

> Exercise is meat for some and poison for others. And the others are usually over 40. Personally, I can't even take exercise diluted. I prefer mine in a rocking chair. The tips of my toes leave the floor every now and then—only because a stiff breeze had come up from the southwest to rock the chair (and me in it.) I just happen to be in the wind's way—that's how I get my exercise. I most certainly do not go around looking for it. That would upset my whole philosophy of existence.

For years I have advocated the rocking chair as being more than a decorative piece of furniture. I have advised patients of its usefulness for taking moderate exercise and as an instrument which allows you to let off steam when you get worried or upset. A home isn't a home without a rocking chair. Especially when there are a few people over 40 around. For a long time mine was a lost voice in the wilderness as I extolled the value and comfort of this wonderful invention.

How comforting, then, to be reading lately about others who are aware of its enticing promises. For example, a favorite columnist writes, "Ten minutes in a rocking chair is better therapy for frazzled nerves at the day's end than any number of pills or potions."

Want more scientific proof? I have come across an article in a medical journal in which a doctor says that sitting in a rocking chair (and rocking) is beneficial to the overall circulation and of special value to that of the legs. Our medical colleagues in Canada recognize the rocking chair's qualities. Dr. R. C. Swan, of Sundridge, Ontario, points out that "inactivity is a great danger in aging persons. . . . But the rocking chair allows all but the most feeble to engage in limited exercise in any weather; it encourages return of venous blood and aids circulation; stimulates muscle tone and encourages supple joints; helps avoid lung congestion, and toward night encourages sleep by repetitive and sedative effects."

For you lazy folks, especially, what better way to keep moving than by sitting down and doing it? And for you who go into tantrums and fly into rages, who bang walls and throw the furniture around, get yourself a rocker whenever you feel such a spell coming on. Plunk yourself down and let the comforting arms of the ol' rockin' chair enfold you. Then push away and go lickety-split for five or ten minutes. Don't be surprised if your anger and distress disappear as if by magic. No tranquilizer could possibly work so quickly and efficiently.

However, forgetting about rages and tantrums, the rocking chair is good to sit in any time. At the end of a hard day filled with worries, a fifteen-minute session in your rocking chair brings relief and surcease for the heart and mind.

I believe that twiddling your thumbs as you sit rocking quietly in a rocking chair is all the exercise many heart patients require after 40. Nevertheless, I am not against sensible exercise for those over 40. For example, years ago I wrote that each new decade after 40 demands a new restriction in physical exertion. If you want a workout because you like sports, nine holes of golf on a weekday or eighteen on Sunday should be sufficient. Tennis? A set or two of singles with a person of your age and ability—or, better still, doubles with three other former champions. Walking, fishing, bowling, gardening? Fine, but all in moderation and stopping short this side of extreme fatigue.

Your heart is not an organ that needs to be pampered, but it expects a square deal. Even the innocent game of tennis may be potentially dangerous for those past 40. For example, consider this report which appeared in the *Journal of the American Medical Association:*

> The physicians specializing in sports medicine met at their annual conference last December in the city of Munich. Some 150 specialists participated. . . . A group of researchers from the University of Erlangen, West Germany, instructed the audience that competitive sports, like tennis, may be quite dangerous to people past the age of 40; even those who started playing tennis at a young age and trained incessantly are exposed to a variety of sudden cardiovascular and musculoskeletal complications if they overdo strenuous exercise.

Still, many exercisers look upon physical laziness as an eccentricity. A recent press report stated that Sir Compton Mackenzie, author of one hundred books, died at 89. His last book was published on his eighty-eighth birthday. "An eccentric," the report went on, "Mackenzie's motto was 'Never stand when you can sit. Never sit when you can lie down. Never walk when you can ride.' "

Eccentric? Why? Because he had an aversion to jogging or doing pushups? Why don't exercise fanciers let a physically lazy man die in peace? Why slur a dead man who can't get up (and probably wouldn't even if he could) to defend his good name?

Yes, I come to your side, Sir Compton Mackenzie. If you had lived to be 100 instead of 89, it's likely a sweating, self-righteous overexerter would say, "If you'd exercised more you would have lived longer."

Satchel Paige, now in his eighties is as famous for his prescriptions for good health and long life as he is for his remarkable career as a pitcher. I don't agree with his dictum, "Avoid running at all times." I'm not as antiexercise as all that. However, I subscribe to another famous saying of his: "Keep the juices flowing by jangling around gently as you move."

How better to "jangle around gently" after a hard day than by relaxing in a rocker?

SEDATIVES AS CRUTCHES

If you have been nervous and sleepless, your own doctor will have to determine how long you will need to take sedatives. It will all depend on your underlying condition. Some need to wear crutches only for a day or two; others, for months. A temporary emergency will require sedatives only for a short while. However, if you suffer from chronic anxiety, or from some other ailment that lasts longer, your doctor will prescribe larger amounts of the sedative.

Here are some practical suggestions about the use of sedatives. Better not take them for minor distress; save them for relief of severe symptoms. If you have been nervous, it makes good sense to have a complete examination to determine the reason, before relying on sedatives.

Do not overdose yourself. If prescribed doses make you too sleepy and unresponsive to daily tasks, inform your doctor. A lower dosage of the drug may be effective. Remember that taking barbiturates for long periods may make you dependent on them. If your doctor prescribes only a small quantity, do not try to obtain barbiturates on your own. Don't mix barbiturates with other drugs, especially alcohol. When taking such drugs, drive carefully, or not at all. Keep your medicine out of reach of children. Dispose old medicines.

I tell people to consider sedatives and tranquilizers to be used as canes while they are limping through a minor emotional problem and to consider sleeping pills as crutches to get them over the rough spots. Too many who need such help refuse to accept it because they are afraid of "dope," afraid of getting the habit, afraid that these medicines may actually harm them. I try to reassure them by saying that these drugs are harmless when taken under a doctor's supervision, but only harmful when self-prescribed. Some patients who have become addicted to sedatives and sleeping pills manage to get more pills by seeing a new doctor and having him prescribe the medication.

Under such conditions I would admit that it's like taking dope. Remember these no-no's: Don't bootleg pills. Don't take them on your own. Don't buy over-the-counter sleeping pills without your doctor's knowledge. Be thankful for sleeping pills, but respect them.

If you have become addicted your doctor will explain how to take less of the medication gradually, so you will not suffer withdrawal symptoms. I've seen some patients go into convulsions when they suddenly stopped their sedatives and sleeping pills. Keep remembering that sedatives are especially dangerous when mixed with alcohol and when driving a car. Asleep at the wheel, many have had serious accidents.

"Dear Dr. Steincrohn," one patient wrote,

> I am not a book borrower, but I am a pill borrower. I'm referring to sleeping pills. For about six months I was on barbiturates prescribed by my doctor. I bought them from the drugstore on prescription. At my last visit a few months ago, the doctor refused to write any more prescriptions. He said he did not want me to be taking them for the rest of my life.
> I decided to leave him for another doctor. But instead of spending money for an unnecessary examination, I began to borrow a few pills here and there from my friends. Most of them take sleeping pills. One, who is my constant companion, gets all the sleeping pills she needs. Her doctor keeps prescribing for her. Am I harming myself?

Your experience tempts me to quote statistics or jump up on a platform and give a lecture on the potential dangers of the barbiturate habit. In this case, I'll combine the two. I hope I can convince you that sedatives aren't always innocuous.

It's true that you are not alone. About 180 million prescriptions for mood-changing drugs were filled by U. S. pharmacists in 1967. Sixty-five percent were for sedative drugs; 31 percent were for barbiturates. About 30 million Americans were on tranquilizers of one sort or another. (There are at least fifty different commercial brands of sleep-producing barbiturates on the market.)

But the next time you swallow barbiturates without medical supervision remember they are dangerous. Many cases have been reported in which the alcohol and barbiturate levels in the blood were singly insufficient to produce fatality, but the combination did.

If and when it comes time to withdraw the drug entirely and suddenly, the severe withdrawal may resemble delerium tremens. The patient may have restlessness, agitation, muscle cramps, nausea, convulsions, and delusions. Death can result from withdrawal as from overuse.

Barbiturates can be dangerous whether you borrow, beg, or steal them—or take them legitimately. My suggestion is to talk it all over with your doctor and confess your borrowing habits.

13

CONTROL THE KILLER DISEASES

Whether you are a jogger or one allergic to exercise, you can't possibly be fit if you have unsuspected high blood pressure. High blood pressure is a continuing challenge because millions of Americans do not suspect they have it. According to Irvine H. Page, M. D., of the Cleveland Clinic, an authority on hypertension: "Hypertension with its regular accompaniment, atherosclerosis, [clogged arteries] is the most important numerically of all diseases in the United States." Therefore, you can understand why there is urgent need to bring it under control.

Statistics often repeated may become tiring, but to be effective, a nail has to be hammered and hammered. Left to stick out, all it's good for is hanging your hat on. So it is with these quotes from authorities trying to solve the major problem of high blood pressure. Perhaps if you read them often enough you may be convinced to try to save your own life. Remember it's your heart I'm writing about.

In a talk given at a meeting sponsored by the Renal and Cardiology divisions of the Department of Medicine of the Johns Hopkins School of Medicine on October 3, 1974, William P. Castelli, M. D., director of laboratories for the National Heart and Lung Institute in Framingham, Massachusetts, made some pertinent observations. He said that high blood pressure (HBP) plays a predominant role in the "heart attack epidemic" in the United States. He said that HBP is one of three major contributing factors in the epidemic. The other two are high cholesterol levels and cigarette smoking.

Surveys, including the Framingham Study which was begun twenty-five years ago, have shown that by the age of 60, every fifth man and every seventeenth woman will have suffered a heart attack. Studies have also shown that HBP is a causative factor in strokes.

Dr. Castelli said that the Framingham study has shown that every eighth man between the ages of 40 and 44 will have a heart attack during the next fourteen years. A person's chances of suffering an attack increase with age, the study shows, and during a fourteen-year period, heart attacks will strike every sixth man in the 45 to 49 age group, every fifth man in the 50 to 54 age group, and every fourth man older than 55. In the Framingham study, 75 percent of the people suffering strokes and heart failure had been victims of untreated high blood pressure. "And so we feel," Dr. Castelli said,

> that it's important for doctors to identify the people who are running high blood pressures and bring them under control. Because I think it's fairly well known that if you treat hypertension, you reduce the risk of stroke by a fifth. Seven-eighths of the high blood pressure victims in this country go untreated. Hypertension pervades our whole society. Eventually every third man, and four out of ten women in our country, develop HBP. . . . But most of these people don't have symptoms, and they're not going to go to their doctors, because they feel okay. The only way you're going to find these people is to go out and stomp around and in some way get them to come in for a blood pressure measurement.

The Framingham Study began twenty-five years ago using a random sample of half the town's 10,000 people between 30 and 62. Initial information was taken from each participant, and follow-ups were made at two-year intervals.

Are you convinced of the importance of knowing your blood pressure reading? Or, do you still say, "Why bother with a blood pressure checkup?" If the latter, you'd better accept the nomination: you are a candidate for early extinction. You can only hope that you lose the election.

Patients who want to make a personal contribution to their health and well-being and buy their own blood pressure machines to take their readings at home between visits get mixed responses from their doctors. Physicians often feel that this practice makes patients too conscious of their blood pressure and might even elevate their readings. Other physicians, however, are coming around to the opinion that taking blood pressure readings at home will help both doctor and patient.

I believe that patients and their family members should be taught to record their own blood pressures at home. It should preferably be taken by another family member because recording one's own pressure may not elicit a true reading. If we hope to prevent the complications of hypertension (stroke, heart attack, kidney trouble), it is important that high blood pressure be detected early and supervised constantly. Regularly monitoring the blood pressure in the home can greatly improve such a program.

The diabetic patient is taught how to examine his urine for sugar, and such cooperation has proved effective for better management. The patient with hypertension, or the one who wonders whether he has it, should not wait for symptoms to warn of danger. Some never have symptoms, although others complain of dizziness, ringing in the ears, vertigo, headaches, or palpitation.

Keeping a record of your blood pressure readings at home should help the doctor evaluate the actions of drugs he prescribes. Pressure readings taken at home are often lower than those taken in the doctor's office. As a result, you may require a lower dosage.

Once the diagnosis of hypertension has been made, you should know how you and your doctor can hope to control it. Here are some practical considerations:

• Keep your weight down. Remember that obesity is the enemy of the arteries.

• Prepare yourself for the long-distance race, not for the sprint. High blood pressure, however mild it may seem to be, is a condition that requires observation and treatment for the rest of your life. Only in this way will you be taking an important measure to save your heart.

• Discard the salt shaker. Hypertensives treat themselves with one hand tied behind the back if they continue to take salt.

• Exercise moderately. Walk, swim, bowl, or play golf or tennis in moderation.

• Learn to relax. Daily naps help.

• Remove the word "hurry" from your vocabulary. It is a dirty word.

• Have your blood pressure checked at regular intervals. Do not get into the habit of cancelling visits to your doctor. Learn how to take your blood pressure at home.

• Consider your bathroom scales an important aid. Approximately 40 percent of all overweight patients are also hypertensive. The increased death rate of obese patients can be blamed, to a large extent, on their hypertension.

• Are you diabetic? Help your doctor control it.

• The same for gout.

• Do you take the pill? John H. Laragh, M.D., former Professor of Clinical Medicine at Columbia-Presbyterian Medical Center in New York City, had this to say about the pill and hypertension:

> When a woman of child-bearing age comes in with hypertension, one of the questions we ask is if she is on the pill or any other form of estrogen therapy. The preferred treatment for a woman who becomes hypertensive on the pill is discontinuation of that form of contraception. It must be pointed out though, that the pressure doesn't revert to its normal level right away. We find that most hypertensive women who go off the pill become normotensive in two to four months. . . . What we think is that any woman whose blood pressure shows a convincing, even if slight, trend upward after she has gone on the pill or any woman on the pill who retains a lot of fluid, should probably use another method of contraception. . . . But I'm certainly not going to say the pill shouldn't be used. That would be a major error.

Why are all these methods I've outlined so important in managing hypertension? Because studies indicate that morbidity and mortality are directly related to the level of blood pressure. In men between the ages of 35 and 45, the twenty-year mortality rate is five times higher in individuals with a blood pressure of 160/100 than in those with a blood pressure below 140/90. The Framingham studies show that the risk in patients with even a modest elevation of blood pressure is six times greater than in the normotensive population for congestive failure, three to five times greater for stroke, and two to three times greater for fatal heart attack. Life expectancy is progressively shortened the higher the level of blood pressure.

How effective are the antihypertensive drugs in preventing complications? The results of one study indicated that the risk of developing a major cardiovascular complication over a five-year period was reduced from 55 percent to 18 percent by treatment with antihypertensive drugs.

Each patient responds differently to drug treatment. We want to control the HBP with a minimum of adverse reactions. It's often necessary for the doctor to try various drugs or combinations at different dose levels until the best effect is obtained. Try not to be impatient during this period of experimentation. Charles L. Curry, M.D., Chief of the cardiovascular division of Freedmens Hospital in Washington, D.C., put it well when he said, "Why don't patients take their medication? It's kind of nebulous—something in human nature that makes people not want to fasten seat belts or quit smoking in spite of the fact they know of the dangers. You have to be very compulsive to take medicine every day. What you *know* about hypertension and what you *do* about it are not necessarily the same thing."

Before beginning a life-long course of drug treatment, the patient who has an apparently mildly elevated BP should be seen on at least three separate visits to learn whether his blood pressure is persistently elevated. Also, special studies should be made of the extent of any organic damage to the fundi (back of the eyes), brain, heart, and kidneys. Since specific drug programs require a detailed supervision by your doctor, I will not even attempt to go into a description of antihypertensive therapy except to mention some of the drugs commonly used.

Five antihypertensive medications, singly or in combination, will control the majority of HBP problems. They are reserpine, alpha methyldopa, guanethidine, thiazid diuretics, and hydralazine.

Reserpine, alpha methyldopa, and guanethidine act by depressing the activity of the sympathetic nervous system. The thiazid diuretics act by lowering blood pressure through sodium and extracellular fluid. And Hydralazine acts by dilating the arterioles (smaller arteries) by a direct action on the vascular smooth muscle of the arteries themselves.

This potent choice of ammunition to bring down high blood pressure requires careful manipulation in each patient for the best results. In general, the purpose should be to use as few different drugs as possible. Some patients have reactions to the medication. Some who take reserpine may develop depression, anxiety, loss of appetite, and insomnia. The alert physician will discontinue the drug and substitute something else, and the symptoms will disappear. It is at such times that it is necessary to carry out a therapeutic trial to determine the most effective treatment. As I said, don't be discouraged; the major reason for poor control of high blood pressure is the patient's failure to continue the medication.

Do you rock up and back on your heels and toes evidently proud that you don't scare easily? Then surely, what I am about to say is for you. It may help convince you that you may be walking around with a bomb in one of your pockets. Unfortunately, it may not bulge and warn you of danger; it doesn't tick. It gives no warning of dire things to come: stroke, heart attack, kidney disease. You don't know what will set it off.

You pat your pockets. Nothing there. You never felt better, no headaches, no dizziness. Why worry about high blood pressure? What bomb?

Hypertension is notorious for being untrustworthy. It is the insidious disease. It is not frank and honest. It's like a con man who looks you straight in the eye and shakes your hand warmly and vigorously. He hides his evident wish to fleece you. Therefore, you must live in distrust until you check him out. So you must do with hypertension. Is your blood pressure your friend or enemy?

The odds are one in nine that you have high blood pressure. And if you do have it, the odds are that you don't know it. According to the American Medical Association, hypertension is the primary cause of about 60,000 deaths each year in the United States. It also plays an important role in the more than 1.5 million heart attacks and strokes that Americans suffer each year. One estimate is that of the 23 million who have high blood pressure, at least half do not even suspect they have it. Do you?

All patients should have blood pressure readings on every visit to the doctor, whether the visit is for a Pap smear, an eye checkup, an itch, or a pain. Only by such mass screening will we discover, early, that the unsuspecting patient suffers from hypertension.

A 48-year-old friend of our family broke her leg in a skiing accident. She hadn't had an examination in years. The orthopedist who treated her never took her blood pressure reading. About three months later she decided to have a physical checkup. Her systolic blood pressure was over 200.

Mass screening in mobile vans or at shopping centers or in bank lobbies may be helpful in detecting hypertension otherwise overlooked, but the ideal place for examination is the doctor's office. On a national scale, however, success depends on doctors routinely measuring every patient's blood pressure, regardless of the complaint. Even specialists who do not treat cardiovascular problems should make routine blood pressure checks when they examine a patient. The task is to find, treat, and motivate, but first of all to find.

What is especially sad about the hundreds of thousands of cases of slow suicide is that the treatment of high blood pressure has been demonstrated to be successful in prolonging life. As former secretary of the Department of Health, Education and Welfare, Elliot L. Richardson said,

> Hypertension is a problem with which the state of the art and science of modern medicine already has demonstrated an impressive ability to cope. Yet millions of our fellow citizens are not getting the full benefit of this medical knowledge and skill. Hypertension can be brought under control by proven treatment which is neither unduly hazardous, expensive, or complicated.

Patients are often confused about what to do regarding salt intake in their diet. One said, "My doctor told me that my blood pressure is only moderately high. He said it isn't necessary for me to go on a strict low salt diet, but another doctor said it's important to cut down on salt." According to Lewis K. Dahl, M.D., chief of staff at Brookhaven National Laboratory, Upton, New York, "For fifteen years or more I have been treating so-called benign hypertension in the belief that a physician should not stand idly by in the presence of serious illness." Although Dr. Dahl believes there is no single best treatment, his view is that it should include some restriction on salt intake: "We know beyond a doubt that in the presence of salt restriction, all other treatment approaches are more effective." Dr. Dahl also believes that if an individual has what might be called a genetic predisposition to high blood pressure, high salt intake may be the triggering factor in its development.

Use the following rule of thumb for attaining a low salt diet that is both simple and effective: never add salt to food during preparation or at the table; avoid milk and milk products; avoid all processed foods except fruits and juices, and even here examine the labels.

In my own practice, I have walked the middle road, applying moderation, as always. When a wife says to me, "I can't get Jim to cut down on his salt," naturally Jim would get a short lecture from me on the possible harmful effects of salt. However, when patients said that they did not use salt on their food at the table and that it was not used in cooking, I did not make too many further restrictions— unless their blood pressure was extremely high or there were heart complications.

If you have high blood pressure, no matter how high, respect the potential dangers of salt intake.

Here are three provocative case histories:

FIRST PATIENT: My blood pressure is low. For six months I have visited the doctor for a weekly liver shot. But my pressure isn't any higher. Only 100. I'm sore all over—and in my pocketbook, too. Since I feel well otherwise, I wonder why I should have to be getting shots every week. Do you advise such treatment?

SECOND PATIENT: I am 36 years old. I have spent a great part of my life fighting low blood pressure. I've never been able to live a normal life because of it. Over the years, I've changed doctors many times, hoping that treatment would change with each doctor. I have been taught how to administer my own shots: B12, crude liver, and B complex weekly. I am unable to work. I require days of complete bed rest. I think the low pressure must be affecting my heart. Yet I have been told by each doctor that there is very little to be done for low pressure except what I am doing. Is there any other special advice you can give me?

THIRD PATIENT: I have low blood pressure. My doctor says it isn't serious, but then why did he mention it in the first place? I admit I feel all right. I have no pains, aches, or indigestion. However, I do get tired occasionally. I am 38 years old. Is it likely the pressure will go up to normal sometime in the future? I don't consider myself to be a worrywart. However, I think you will agree that it's natural for me to be concerned about blood pressure that is low.

How high is up? How low is down? I'm not being facetious. These are questions that must be answered before we can make proper estimates of blood pressure readings. Consider some figures: 140 to 150 (systolic) over 90 or less (diastolic) are accepted limits of the upper normal blood pressure range. Of course, much depends on age, weight, and where and when readings are taken.

But what is abnormally low pressure? Is it a systolic of 120, 110, or 90? There is no definite point of demarcation. A man who has come through a siege of chronic illness following a major operation or a serious heart attack may have a systolic blood pressure of 100 that is not too low. After a full recuperation, it may stay that way or rise to 120-140 systolic without need for medication. However, what about a woman who complains of weakness which borders on complete exhaustion, who is underweight, and has lost appetite and strength, and whose systolic blood pressure is between 70 and 80? Examination shows she suffers from Addison's disease, a weakness in the adrenal glands. In her case, hypotension is abnormal. Proper medication with adrenal hormones brings up her pressure and dissipates most of her symptoms.

There is no valid reason to treat low blood pressure unless we discover it is due to something specific, such as Addison's disease; severe anemia; or a long-standing, debilitating disease. Patients whose blood pressure plummets in shock from sudden loss of blood or during a heart attack should also be treated for low blood pressure.

Too many normal patients are being "shot up" for hypotension, however. I am one who does not believe that liver and vitamin shots raise chronic low blood pressure, and I know of no medication or other treatment which is effective in raising hypotension to normal pressure levels over a long period of time.

I suggest that people stop being so low-blood-pressure conscious. A systolic pressure of 100 is normal for many people. I have known some athletes whose resting pressures never went much above 90. So why try to raise pressure at all? People too apprehensive about having low blood pressure should be thankful: it spares the heart. According to insurance company statistics, you will live longer if your blood pressure is on the low side.

Why be a pincushion for unnecessary, painful, and expensive jabs of the needle? Why be a willing target for shots? If your doctor insists that you need such treatment for your low blood pressure, he may be right. But personally, I believe you would be better off asking for consultation. Ask for another opinion before submitting to target practice on your nether end.

DIABETES AND CORONARIES

Man is an enigma to himself, a perpetual question mark, who occasionally straightens up into an exclamation point, but invariably ends as a period. He has unconsciously loosened his grip on life. The choice varies: obesity, hypertension, heart disease, chronic alcoholism, overexertion, abnormal tension, tobacco?

The ways of slow suicide are many. One threat we must not overlook is diabetes mellitus. This is one of the major and most effective weapons of self-destruction.

Diabetes doesn't invariably announce its arrival, but neither does high blood pressure, coronary disease, or other killers. Chronic illness does not always warn, and diabetes is one of the sneaky diseases. A 48-year-old man thought he was healthy until he fractured his wrist in an auto accident. His doctor did a routine test on his urine. Result? Brick red. Later a blood sugar test confirmed diabetes as the diagnosis. Yet this man had no symptoms which might have warned him before the accident.

Too many depend upon certain well-known symptoms of diabetes to guard against the disease. Excessive hunger, weight loss, excessive thirst and urination, weakness, and easy tiring are the classic symptoms, but by the time they show up the disease may have been present for months or years. Less common, but earlier warnings are changes in vision, intense itching (especially in vaginal area), slow healing of cuts, unusual drowsiness, and burning sensations and pains in fingers and toes.

One estimate is that there are at least 50 million prediabetic patients in the United States. Even if this number is exaggerated, it should give you an inkling of the overwhelming nature of the problem. Your job is to recognize some of the red lights lit up along the track, to slow down when warnings come and proceed cautiously. Early diagnosis is essential if you want the odds in your favor. Here are some tips that may save you from committing slow suicide. These are some clinical features that may suggest the possibility of diabetes.

Family history. Any family involvement with diabetes mellitus should make you extremely cautious. If there is diabetes on both sides of the family you should have a glucose tolerance test (GTT). Even though your parents may not have had it, you should not ignore the history of a diabetic uncle, aunt, or grandparent. But if a brother, sister, or parent has diabetes the chances are one in five that, as an adult, you have an abnormal GTT.

Trouble with vision. Have you noticed that your vision has become blurred lately? You can't see as well as you used to? You blame it entirely on being middle-aged, and therefore expect it. The trouble may be more than lies in the calendar itself. In some patients, cataracts are the first warning of diabetes. Some opthalmologists miss the underlying disease by not ordering a GTT. Other reasons for a glucose tolerance examination are such eye changes as retinal hemorrhages, retinal detachment, or glaucoma. In the middle-aged and older, gradual or sudden trouble in seeing are red lights waving madly as warnings of diabetes.

Nerve signals. I have made an early diagnosis of diabetes in a number of patients whose only complaints were some form of neuritis. Their burning sensations and pains in the hands and legs had been attributed to trouble with the circulation. Examination of the blood sugar revealed the true cause. Some patients complained of sudden numbness and weakness in the arms or legs. A few had spinal cord trouble producing ulcers of the foot. Some had symptoms such as an inability to completely empty the bladder. Any unusual, inexplicable nerve problem should make us think of diabetes as a possibly contributing cause.

Kidney Disease. Stubborn urinary tract infections that resist treatment should make us suspicious that this pyelonephritis is tied in with diabetes. A condition causing renal failure called Kimmelstiel-Wilson disease may be one of the first signs of diabetes mellitus.

Obesity. If you are overweight, beware. Although being obese is not in itself a direct cause of diabetes, if you carry around excess poundage for years, it is not unlikely that this will precipitate the onset of diabetes. Many diabetics are overweight.

Hypertension. Although there is no direct tie-in here either, it is becoming evident that the hypertensive is a more likely candidate for having diabetes than the one with normal blood pressure.

Arteriosclerosis. Whatever your age, if you have evidence of arteriosclerosis (calcification of the aorta or other large vessels as seen on the X ray) or coronary or vascular cerebral disease, think of the possibility of diabetes. The earlier that arteriosclerosis comes on, the more liable that diabetes will be found. For example, if you are fifty when you show undisputed evidence of arteriosclerosis, tests will show you have a 50 percent likelihood of having diabetes.

Skin signs. Become suspicious if you have crops of boils that recur; carbuncles; ulcers of the leg that do not heal; infected corns or toenails; severe itching around the vagina or anus.

Pregnancy. Babies weighing over nine pounds sometimes indicate an overlooked diabetes in mother or child. A condition called "transient hyperglycemia or glycosuria" is too often ignored by physicians when found in pregnant women. Yet such patients should have observation for possible diabetes long after pregnancy is over. It has also been found that spontaneous abortions, premature labor, and preeclampsia occur more frequently in mothers who are prediabetic or diabetic.

Laboratory findings. Any patient who has had a single elevation of blood sugar or shown a trace of glucose in the urine should have further tests. Too many times such findings are explained away as being a part of such problems as myocardial infarction, stroke, or infection. Further study will often show that diabetes is also present. Suspicion should also be raised if a person has an elevation of blood cholesterol or blood triglycerides; if the electrocardiogram of a patient under 50 shows only the possible presence of heart disease; if there is abnormally high uric acid content in the blood; and if X rays indicate gall bladder disease. Gout or gall bladder infection are often present in older diabetics. Even hypoglycemia should put you on the alert; sometimes this is the forerunner or a partner of diabetes.

Of all the warnings, obesity is overlooked more than the others. Dr. Jesse Roth of the National Institute of Health, Bethesda, Maryland, has said what you should know by now, that obesity is one of the most common diseases. Obese people frequently have high levels of blood sugar. The proper way to manage an obese diabetic is to treat his obesity, and a majority of diabetics are obese before they are diabetic. If an obese diabetic is placed on a fasting diet instead of on medication, "you find he gets a better response because blood sugar and insulin decrease and resistance decreases."

There is no specific treatment—diet or insulin—outlined in this chapter. The one who tries to save you from inadvertantly plunging over the side of a cliff leaves the rest of the management of your life to your personal physician. As diabetes mellitus is a continuing problem, it is he and you together who will have to solve it as questions arise. There is no blanket treatment for diabetes nor for any disease.

What I have been saying may sound quite foreboding, but I think you should know that, properly treated, diabetes doesn't usually cause such complications as trouble with vision, artery disease, or other trying burdens. Only those who do not respect diabetes as a potentially harmful condition fall into the trap of disregarding early diagnosis and observing a proper diet and insulin treatments, if necessary.

Years ago a child with diabetes had little chance of living into adulthood. Now, with ordinary, good care he can live his life in a normal way without too many restrictions. In fact, it is common knowledge that some of our most well-known athletes in baseball, hockey, and tennis have been diabetics for years and have admitted it in writing and on TV and radio without detriment to their careers. They are not alone. The same is true for many of our prominent business and professional men and women. Sometimes the disease is so mild that it can be controlled by diet alone. At other times, it is controlled by taking insulin. Once the diagnosis has been made, however, noncooperation in treatment becomes dangerous. Play the game. Follow the rules. Otherwise, you may suffer needless penalties.

Unless you are aware of your weaknesses and strengths—and your doctor's weaknesses and strengths—you are a potential candidate for a coronary attack. Such knowledge is the most potent antidote for the chronic poisons of self-destruction.

In my experience, intelligence does not guarantee good health care. I recall a judge, who was also a Ph.D. and a recipient of many honorary degrees from colleges, who died suddenly in his early fifties of a heart attack. He had suffered from obesity and untreated diabetes for years. For three months before his fatal illness, he stopped by a drugstore in the neighborhood of the courthouse daily to take a bicarb mixture "for this darn stomach of mine." He could not conceive that the "gas" was a by-product of a failing heart. Otherwise, it is likely he would have sought medical help earlier.

Too many die before their time. Here are some additional facts which will help neutralize the threat of diabetes if you have coronary heart disease. Heart disease is more common in diabetics, especially in females. Under 60, in the nondiabetic population, the rate of coronary disease is about three males to one female. In the diabetic population the male to female ratio is 1:1. If you happen to have high blood pressure along with diabetes, the severity of coronary disease is greater.

It's important to regulate diabetes; uncontrolled, it may increase fatty acid metabolism and cause acidosis, a water and electrolyte imbalance, and an inability to metabolize glucose. It's important, too, to use insulin and the other antidiabetic drugs with care; otherwise the result may be hypoglycemia and myocardial infarction.

Diabetic patients often ask if they can withstand bypass coronary surgery. The answer is yes. Indications for the operation are similar to those who do not have diabetes.

Statistical evidence indicates that diabetes exerts deleterious effects on arteries. For example, juvenile diabetics may show signs of atherosclerosis as early as the third, fourth, or fifth decade. In nondiabetics, such changes appear later—in the fifth, sixth, and seventh decades. Therefore, it makes good sense for the diabetic to have early treatment for the purpose of having normal sugar and fat metabolism. This may retard the onset of atherosclerosis.

We must not overtreat the diabetic—not try to obtain an absolutely normal blood sugar. Your level should not be allowed to fall below 150 mg/ml (millileters) and the urine should contain a 1+ sugar reading. Otherwise, your blood sugar may fall too low and produce an infarction in the heart muscle.

Oral antidiabetic drugs can be used, but with caution. There's still some evidence that such drugs may harm the heart. Remember that other arteries than those in the heart may be threatened by uncontrolled diabetes. We hope to forestall complications in your kidney and eye arteries.

What this all adds up to is that diabetes mellitus, like hypertension, obesity, and tobacco, is one of the four rampaging enemies that threatens to cut your lifelines unless you stay alert.

HYPOGLYCEMIA

He is a completely frustrated patient. He has been examined by three of the finest heart specialists in his city. All, he says, have given him the A-OK on his health; yet he continues to have these frequent attacks of dizziness and nervousness. Sometimes he gets severe headaches and thinks he is going to pass out. With it, he is disturbed by chest pains which he thinks are due to angina. All the special tests and examinations continue to exonerate his heart. He eats well and sleeps well. He says he doesn't worry except when he has these attacks. He admits to one bad habit: "I smoke at least two packs a day."

The first temptation is to put such a patient in the class of hypochondriacs who are abnormally concerned with themselves, but this man appeared to be a stable person, unemotionally involved with his complaints. Something must be causing him this distress. What might have been overlooked in his previous examinations? As many doctors still remain unconvinced that hypoglycemia is a common cause of many nervous symptoms, I asked him if he had had a glucose tolerance test. The answer was no.

I recalled having read some time before that there have been a few proved cases of hypoglycemia in susceptible persons who were heavy smokers. I have observed a few in my own practice. I fished around for the article and luckily came across it. Written by Maxwell G. Berry, M. D., of Kansas City it appeared in the *Annals of Internal Medicine*. He reported seeing twenty-four patients with tobacco hypoglycemia since 1946. In order of frequency, here are the symptoms noted by these patients: nervousness, dizziness, fatigue, blind staggers, headache, fainting, and cough.

Dr. Berry made the diagnosis of hypoglycemia only in patients who met the following criteria: (1) the use of one or more packages of cigarettes a day (or equivalent), (2) symptoms compatible with the diagnosis of hypoglycemia, (3) blood sugar below 55 mg. per 100 m/l concurrent with the above symptoms, (4) prompt relief by the ingestion or administration of glucose (sugar) at the time symptoms occurred, and (5) complete and permanent relief of symptoms with cessation of smoking.

Symptoms like faintness, dizziness, fatigue, and nervousness sometimes appear in heart patients. It is evident that the diagnosis of hypoglycemia in suspected heart trouble is a welcome finding. This proved to be true in the patient under consideration. Undoubtedly he had low blood sugar. Provocative tests proved it. Within weeks after he discontinued smoking, his symptoms disappeared. Greatly relieved, he admitted that his greatest fear was that he might be suffering from coronary disease.

Occasionally a patient having an attack of hyperventilation will simulate a heart attack. One patient I recall complained suddenly of excessive sweating, nausea, anxiety, palpitation, weakness, and chest pain. The diagnosis of acute myocardial infarction was ruled out by negative blood enzymes studies and negative heart tracings. He recovered quickly after rebreathing into a paper bag to restore proper oxygen and carbon dioxide balance in the blood.

Low blood sugar and hyperventilation—as you are now aware—are only two of the many conditions in the body that may simulate a true heart attack.

Much has been written about how elevated cholesterol and triglycerides are tied in with diabetes and coronary disease. Rather than be sunk in a sea of postulations, all you need to know is that no physical checkup is complete unless your doctor evaluates these fatty substances. If your cholesterol is over 225 or 250, it is too high and needs to be lowered by proper medication and by a diet containing less saturated fats. If the triglycerides are above normal, over 150, then it's important to cut out, or down, drinking and overeating.

Jogging enthusiasts claim that this exercise will lower these blood lipids. But don't depend on it, except for temporary reductions. Remember that exercise is not the cure-all for practically everything that ails you.

MIRACLE PUMP

Plumbers, school teachers, business executives—nearly everyone takes the miracles of the world for granted, and the heart is surely near the top of the list of miracles. Much needless illness and suffering can be avoided if you appreciate nature's miracles, so it is worth learning about your heart.

The heart weighs only about ten ounces, little more than half a pound. Yet, this miniature pump, the size of your fist, ejects about six ounces of blood at each contraction. This adds up to about 5,000 gallons, or twenty tons, every twenty-four hours through approximately 60,000 miles of blood vessels. During twenty-four hours of stress your heart may propel as much as fifty to a hundred tons of blood.

If yours is the average heart, you were alloted approximately 3 billion heartbeats, with perhaps another billion in reserve for stresses and strains.

Your heart is a four-chambered double pump. The right heart receives blood by veins from the rest of the body. It pumps blood through the pulmonary artery to the lungs, where it is freshened with oxygen. After the left heart receives this oxygenated blood, it pumps it through the aorta to your tissues and organs.

Your heart has its own pacemaker, a small sending station in the upper right chamber of the heart. This unit sends out electroniclike impulses at an average rate of seventy beats per minute. These impulses travel down the heart's own nervous system and spread throughout its muscles. Your heart comes closer to being an automatic, tireless engine than any other piece of machinery.

With few exceptions, every other organ in your body can slow down, even come to a standstill. For example, close your eyes for ten minutes, fast for ten days, or hold your breath for ten seconds. Eyes, stomach, and lungs will pick up where they left off. But if the heart stops for ten seconds, it rarely starts again—unless cardiac resuscitation methods have been successful.

In 1628, William Harvey, discoverer of blood circulation said,

> The heart is the beginning of life—it is the heart by whose virtue and pulse the blood is moved, perfected, made apt to nourish, and is preserved from corruption and coagulation; it is the household divinity which, discharging its function, nourishes, cherishes, quickens the whole body, and is indeed the foundation of life, the source of all action.

Call it the miracle worker and you will not be wrong. It is the indefatigable pump which propels blood throughout the body to bring oxygen and nourishment to every one of the billions of cells. It receives its own nourishment from its two coronary arteries and their branches. When one or more of these larger arteries becomes shut off by sludge or thrombus, the patient is said to be suffering an attack of coronary thrombosis. When a part of the heart muscle supplied by the coronary artery involved is thus deprived of its blood supply, that portion dies. It has become "infarcted."

The welfare of your entire body depends upon the health of its heart pump and the intricate system of arteries and veins, the cardiovascular system, that are the conveyor-belt of life-giving material. This complex of living tissue is intrinsically sturdy and resistant to insult, but eventually it will rise up in revolt against any way of life that threatens to weaken it.

For example, such poisonous habits as overeating, smoking, alcoholism, over or underexercising, living with chronic resentment, excessive stress, underrelaxing, inability to control emotions, all tend to undermine the cardiovascular system. To practice these habits is to invite death, to commit slow suicide. It's as simple as that, and the statistics bear this conclusion out.

One estimate is that 28 million Americans have some form of serious heart and blood vessel disease. About 23 million suffer from hypertension; about 4 million have coronary heart disease; 1.75 million have rheumatic heart disease; and 1.5 million suffer from stroke.

In 1972 slightly over one million died from heart and blood vessel diseases. Of this total, heart attack was responsible for about 683,000 deaths. And yet, in most cases, heart disease can be prevented or cured. Almost never is a heart attack "sudden." Coronary artery disease builds up for years. Its progenitor is atherosclerosis, and it is most common in those who have ignored the risk factors I have already enumerated.

I call your heart the miracle worker because it is so indefatigable. It begins to pump months before you are born and continues, without interruption, for every succeeding second, hour, and year of your life, day and night. It brings oxygen to every cell of your body and removes carbon dioxide. It supplies nourishment to the tissues, including the necessary hormones. It is essential for normal tissue repair and growth.

However, like most miracles, the heart is soon taken for granted—until symptoms call attention to it. For example, if blood supply to the brain is cut off as little as three or four seconds, lightheadedness warns of trouble with the circulation. If supply is cut off for ten or fifteen seconds, unconsciousness supervenes. If cut off for three or four minutes, there may be irreversible brain damage.

Your heart's function is dependent upon perfect coordination of heart beats that originate in the sinoauricular node situated in the right auricle (atrium). This is the heart's natural pacemaker. It is influenced by hormones and nerves. The electrical impulse quickly shifts to another station below called the atrio-ventricular (AV) node. Then the impulse quickly travels through two other branches of specialized muscle tissue called the right and left bundle branches. This is followed by the contractions and relaxations of the heart (systole and diastole). All this is dependent on perfect coordination between heart valves (opening and closing at the right time) as blood flows to and from the lungs, to and from the rest of the body.

Like a crown atop the head of a king, the coronary arteries assert themselves. When they are open to the normal passage of blood, all is well in the kingdom of man. When they become occluded and impede the life-giving nourishment the heart itself needs, comes chaos and the threat of extinction.

EARLY WARNING SIGNALS

About one in ten supposedly healthy men and women over 45 who have come to me for routine yearly physical checkups have evinced ECG signs of previous heart damage. Unaware of danger, they had kept on working and fortunately survived. I have asked them to try to remember anything "different" they have experienced during the previous year. Any gas under the chest? Any extreme shortness of breath on climbing stairs or while playing eighteen holes of golf? Any slight "indigestion" they have attributed to overeating or to spoiled food? Any jaw pain? Any discomfort down an arm? A few recalled some disturbance, but most said they could not recall any suspicious symptoms.

Electrocardiograms and other tests often point the finger at potential danger. Many heart attacks are atypical and lack the signs and symptoms that would put even a first year medical student on guard: excruciating chest pain; excessive perspiration; acute anxiety; weak, irregular pulse, nausea; vomiting; or a sharp fall in blood pressure. One woman told me that had she known of the possibility of a heart attack occurring without pain, four valuable days would not have been lost in treating her 40-year-old husband. Two days after Christmas, he became "uncomfortable" in the chest while driving home. He attributed it to having eaten so much over the holiday. At no time during the next three days did he feel other than slight discomfort.

At last she prevailed upon him to see the family doctor. Although he has passed it all off as a "little indigestion," the doctor ordered an ECG as a precaution. Within the hour he was brought into the hospital, apparently well. A cardiologist was waiting. He was immediately placed in an intensive care coronary unit. The diagnosis: acute coronary thrombosis with myocardial infarction.

"Imagine," she said. "This was about ninety-six hours after his original chest discomfort!" Fortunately, he recovered in spite of his procrastination.

Many attacks are overlooked in exactly this way. Joggers and others who overextend themselves, overworking, overexerting, or overeating, may not know they are having a heart attack because the symptoms aren't severe enough to signal the presence of anything so potentially lethal. Many attacks come on stealthily, wearing masks.

Early diagnosis is essential. Occasionally patients like the one I just mentioned escape the consequences of their procrastinations and evasions, but the future of the coronary patient often depends on what is done during the first few hours or days after the attack. If you are man or woman over forty, become suspicious of any unusual complaints regardless of whether they occur in the chest area or elsewhere. In many patients, distress under the breastbone or in upper abdomen or discomfort that was thought to be the result of a hiatal hernia turned out to be a coronary attack. Don't dismiss unusual dizziness, faintness, indigestion, or shortness of breath, especially if you've never has such complaints at any previous time in your life.

A commercial air pilot once came to me for his checkup a few weeks before he was due for a routine appointment. What brought him in was an unusual pain in his left shoulder. He thought it was an attack of bursitis brought on by painting his house during the previous week. Electrocardiograms indicated he was having a heart attack. Fortunately for him and his passengers, the diagnosis of cardiac infarction was picked up early.

Another patient became anxious about having a heart attack. Within a day, chest eruption revealed that the pain was due to shingles. Other conditions that may stimulate coronary disease are severe anemia, hyperthyroid condition, gall bladder disease, ulcer, and arthritis.

Sometimes early warning symptoms turn out to be something other than a heart attack. A 45-year-old patient wondered if he had stumbled on a reason why he was having more frequent attacks of angina. He noticed pain more often and more severe on days when he was on a high sugar binge, eating lots of chocolates, pies, cakes, and ice cream. On other days, when on an ordinary diet, he felt more comfortable. "Is it possible that too much sugar can produce attacks of heart pain?" he asked. I told him that he might consider himself a codiscoverer of sorts. I had been reading some remarks made at a meeting in Montreal of the International College of Angiology (*Internal Medicine News*, November 1, 1974) that seemed to confirm his theory.

According to Dr. Benjamin P. Sandler of Asheville, North Carolina, the fundamental cause of the anginal syndrome and myocardial infarction is a sharp fall in the blood glucose to hypoglycemic levels. He maintains that "the attacks of angina pectoris and myocardial infarction can be prevented by maintaining patients with angina on a sugar-free, low carbohydrate, high protein diet—with no limitation of fat intake."

Dr. Sandler says that such a diet elevates and stabilizes the blood glucose levels, thereby preventing the sudden sharp falls in the blood glucose that are responsible for the attacks. He recommends between-meal snacks, such as tomato juice, cheese, and cold cuts and points out that the concept that anginal pain is associated with low levels of blood glucose and disturbed mechanisms for regulating blood glucose levels is supported by much clinical and experimental evidence.

In view of these findings, it might be advisable for some angina patients to review their daily food intake. If they are having several anginal attacks during the day, have these attacks been related to an excessive intake of sweets? If so, between-meal protein snacks might be helpful.

I have only one question about Dr. Sandler's observations. If it is true that there is a strong connection between low levels of blood sugar and anginal attacks and myocardial infarctions, why is it that more middle-aged persons with coronary artery disease and hypoglycemia don't suffer more actual heart attacks? Nevertheless, Dr. Sandler's observations are interesting, and they certainly deserve further study.

What should be evident in all this is that the jogger should not take the responsibility of making his or her own diagnosis. I have given several instances which underline the truth that diagnosis is not invariably a simple procedure. It is often complicated by a combination of typical and atypical symptoms and signs that confuse the picture. When in doubt, put yourself in your doctor's hands. This is the most sensible way to forestall slow or sudden suicide by heart disease.

14

ENJOY YOUR WAY TO LONGEVITY

Joggers are vocal and sensitively protective of their addiction to running. They say that anyone who won't believe that jogging is beneficial and exhilarating is moronic, stubbornly negative, and a scare-monger. However, based on what I have observed, I am not discouraged. I have convinced many jogging enthusiasts to turn from immoderation to moderation.

This book contains much specific information that affects everyone's health and fitness, and I am hopeful that it will encourage thousands of formerly reluctant joggers to throw their running shoes into the dark recesses of a closet. And I also envision other thousands who have been on the brink of accepting membership in the jogging craze and who, having read the cautionary advice in the book, will shake their heads and say, "No, jogging's not for me."

Physically lazy persons tend to be content to stay lazy and do not try to transform the overactive to their relaxed way of life. The exercisers, however, are not content unless they try to convert others to their strenuous, masochistic ways. My purpose in this book, as elsewhere, has been to show those given to moderating their physical exertions that an abundance of medical evidence supports them and their so-called lazy ways.

As a practicing physician of many years' experience, I have followed the case histories of the physically lazy and the physically overactive. I have not noted that those who throw their torsos, arms, and legs around are any healthier or more fit than those who get their exercise as a byproduct of the normal exertions of day-to-day living. The periodic eruptions of fitness crazes—for which doctors themselves must bear the responsibility—have not significantly improved the health, productivity, or happiness of their assorted converts.

It is likely, moreover, that underexercisers are in less danger than overexercisers. Although recent medical reports claim that "stress exercising" will so strengthen the heart and circulation that those who engage in jogging, running, and other extreme forms of muscle-stretching and straining will be less likely to have heart attacks and live longer, many medical studies indicate that this theory remains unproved. It has definitely not been born out by my personal experience in practice.

The normal-weighted, relaxed person who does not smoke, drink, or overwork and who lives without too much tension is more likely to be healthier and to live longer than his neighbor who tends to be overweight, jogs, and goes through a variety of bodily contortions.

If you are naturally lazy, do not let anyone convince you to become unnaturally active. If you jog, recognize that you do so at your own risk and that that risk is substantially increased if you fail to observe the precaution of regular, thorough, and expensive cardiac examinations.

A study that followed thousands of college graduates for twenty-five to fifty years after their graduations found that athletes lived no longer than nonathletes. Honor graduates lived longer than athletes. The most important ingredients for longevity seemed to be job satisfaction, intellectual pursuits, and good socioeconomic status.

I know a 45-year-old lawyer who doesn't smoke, drink, overeat, or have any other distinctive bad habits. He said, "I realize that my chances for living longer are enhanced by the way I conduct my life. But, in a way, it's a sacrifice to be so good in order to try to make it to 80. I can think of one other thing I should be doing but don't find the time for—jogging. Would this be another plus in my favor?"

Leaving hypocritical humility aside, I suggested, "Read *Joggermania!* One way or another, that will help you make your decision for or against jogging." At the same time, I told him something that interested him and that I think will interest you, too. It amounted to some observations on longevity.

First I quoted Frederick Loomis, M.D.: "Many years have been added to the average expectation of life, but each individual's fate is still a hazard." This is a way of reminding us that doctors should not wear the mantles of little gods who think they are able to predict you or your neighbor's demise on the basis of your predilection for or against jogging or other exertions. There's much that we still do not know.

Studies do show that some groups of individuals live longer than others. For example, a study of thousands of Protestant ministers found that their mortality rate was about one-third lower than that of all white males of comparable age. As a group, they had lower rates of death from heart disease, stroke, and stomach and lung cancer; they even had fewer accidents and suicides. (I wish investigators had asked how many were joggers and how many were relaxation-minded?)

Symphony conductors live even longer than clergymen. Leopold Stokowski lived to be 95, Arturo Toscanini until 90, Bruno Walter until 85, Walter Damrosch until 88. The mean length of life on a long list of conductors was 73.43 compared to the life expectancy of 68.5 years for the American male. According to Donald H. Atlas, M.D., writing in *Forum on Medicine*, "My own hypothesis, which may explain the prolonged productive life span of this elite group, is based upon their attributes of superior intelligence, unusual talent (perhaps, genius), driving motivation, and most importantly, the sense of fulfillment that comes with world recognition."

The conclusions of an HEW social task force report supports the doctor's belief: "The strongest predictor of longevity was work satisfaction. The second best predictor was overall happiness. These two sociopsychological measures predicted longevity better than a rating by an examining physician of physical functioning, or measure of the use of tobacco, or genetic inheritance."

Perhaps Albert Camus came more quickly to the point: "Without work all life goes rotten. But when work is soulless, life stifles and dies."

William Targ, former editor-in-chief, G. P. Putnam's & Sons, in his book *Indecent Pleasures* (New York: Macmillan,) makes these observations:

> I've observed that dealers in antiquarian goods—for instance, old books, old furniture—outlive the joggers, tennis players, and bicyclists. It's my belief that the longevous individual shuns health foods and exercise and makes sure that no day passes without a modest portion of wine or whiskey. George Bernard Shaw was the exception, but he was bull-headed, he also laughed a good deal, which is the other secret ingredient in the longevity formula.

For the past twenty years, the life expectancy of man has remained on a plateau. Forgetting about the supposed benefits of jogging and other exercise, why aren't we living longer?

Considering the "sense of fulfillment that comes with world recognition" one might suspect that presidents would outlive us all. And indeed, in spite of the burdens of office, President Eisenhower was still in office at the age of 70. Nevertheless, its untrue that presidents outlive the rest of us. The following data from the Statistical Bulletin of Metropolitan Life Insurance Company is informative.

The prognosis for presidents is definitely less favorable than any other group of public officials. "Of the thirty-five deceased presidents, thirteen outlived their expectation of life, while twenty-two fell short. Our longest-lived presidents were John Adams and Herbert C. Hoover, each of whom reached the age of 90."

President John F. Kennedy and James A. Garfield (at 46 and 49 respectively) were both assasinated. Dying of natural causes at 53, James A. Polk was the shortest-lived. The report concluded: "The results of this study indicate that an adverse impact on longevity is exerted by the awesome responsibilities associated with the presidency." This is another way of saying that the Big T, tension, takes its toll.

Admittedly, we have the advantage of many new research laboratories and increased knowledge, but in spite of advancements in medicine, of new procedures, and new complicated diagnostic and therapeutic apparatuses, we've hardly moved an inch towards the objective of longer life. Why? A good question.

We can blame it on diseases of society such as accidents, war, alcoholism, pollution, industrial hazards, and drug abuse, and according to Louis H. Nahum writing in *Connecticut Medicine* (June 1972), "if people fail to accept personal responsibility for their individual health such as obesity, smoking . . .," the average length of life may even decline further. He wrote of the 10 million alcoholics, the 56 million smokers, the obese, the 55,000 deaths on the road yearly, and the 44 million accidents elsewhere.

In reviewing Dr. Nahum's words, I find support for what I've been saying and writing for years—that in one way or another, you and I go about consciously or unconsciously killing ourselves. It's undeniable that too many of us shuffle ourselves off prematurely. Don't you be among those rushing (or jogging) to get off the great stage. Moderate your exertions and habits and, above all, relax and enjoy. This is the soundest prescription any physician can give you for longevity.